The Divine Inspiration of the Bible

The Divine Inspiration of the Bible

A. W. PINK

Tole Publishing
MORGANTOWN, KY 42261

The Divine Inspiration of the Bible first published in 1917; Revised version copyright© 2022 Tole Publishing

All rights reserved. No part of this book may be reproduced, stored in a retrieval system, or transmitted in any form or by any means—electronic, mechanical, photocopying, recording, or otherwise, without written permission from the publisher.

All Scriptures unless otherwise noted are from the KJV: KING JAMES VERSION, public domain.

ISBN: 978-1-948696-52-4

Cover images: All images licensed through Canva; Cover created in Canva

Printed in the United States of America

TOLE PUBLISHING, PO BOX 1098, MORGANTOWN, KY 42261-8411

www.tolepublishing.com

Dedication

*I affectionately inscribe this book to:
my dear Father and Mother,
in grateful appreciation of the fact that
from a child, they taught me to revere
the Holy Scriptures.*

Contents

Introduction   1

1. There Is a Presumption in Favor of the Bible   7
2. The Perennial Freshness of the Bible Bears Witness to its Divine Inspirer   13
3. The Unmistakable Honesty of the Writers of the Bible Attests to its Heavenly Origin   17
4. The Character of its Teachings Evidences the Divine Authorship of the Bible   27
5. The Fulfilled Prophecies of the Bible Bespeak the Omniscience of its Author   40
6. The Typical Significance of the Scriptures Declare Their Divine Authorship   48
7. The Wonderful Unity of the Bible Attests its Divine Authorship   66
8. The Marvelous Influence of the Bible Declares its Super-Human Character   72
9. The Miraculous Power of the Bible Shows Forth That its Inspirer Is the Almighty   76
10. The Completeness of the Bible Demonstrates its Divine Perfection   81
11. The Indestructibility of the Bible Is a Proof that its Author Is Divine   85

12. Inward Confirmation of the Veracity of the   90
    Scriptures
13. Verbal Inspiration   95
14. Application of the Argument   103

Introduction

Christianity is the religion of the Book of books. Christianity is based upon the impregnable rock of Holy Scripture. The starting point of all doctrinal discussions must be the Bible. Upon the foundation of the Divine inspiration of the Bible stands or falls the entire edifice of Christian truth—"*If the foundations be destroyed, what can the righteous do?*" (Psalm 11:3). Surrender the dogma of verbal inspiration and you are left like a rudderless ship on a stormy sea—at the mercy of every wind that blows. Deny that the Bible is, with no qualifications, the very Word of God, and you are left with no ultimate standard of measurement and with no supreme authority. It is useless to discuss any doctrine taught by the Bible until you are prepared to acknowledge, unreservedly, that the Bible is the final court of appeal. Grant that the Bible is a Divine revelation and communication of God's own mind and will to men, and you have a fixed starting point from which we can make an advance into the domain of truth. Grant that the Bible is (in its original manuscripts) inerrant and infallible and you reach the place where the study of its contents is both practicable and profitable.

It is impossible to overestimate the importance of the doctrine of the Divine inspiration of Scripture. This is the strategic center of Christian theology and must be defended at all costs. It is the point at which our satanic enemy is constantly hurling his hellish battalions. Here it was that he had made his first attack. In Eden he asked, "*Yea, hath God said?*" (Genesis 3:1) and today he is pursuing the same tactics. Throughout the ages, the Bible has been the central object of his assaults. Every available weapon in the devil's arsenal has been employed in his determined and ceaseless efforts to destroy the temple of God's truth. In the first days of the Christian era the attack of the enemy was made openly—the bonfire being the chief instrument of destruction—but, in these *last days* the assault is made in a more subtle manner and comes from a more unexpected quarter. The Divine origin of the Scriptures is now disputed in the name of "Scholarship" and "Science," and that, too, by those who profess to be friends and champions of the Bible. Much of the learning and theological activity of the hour are concentrated in the attempt to discredit and destroy the authenticity and authority of God's Word, the result being that thousands of nominal Christians are plunged into a sea of doubt. Many of those who are paid to stand in our pulpits and defend the Truth of God are now the very ones who are engaged in sowing the seeds of unbelief and destroying the faith of those to whom they minister. But these modern methods will prove no more successful in their efforts to destroy the Bible than did those employed in the opening centuries of the Christian era. As well might the birds attempt to demolish the granite rock of Gibraltar by pecking at it with their beaks—"*Forever, O Lord, Thy Word is settled in heaven*" (Psalm 119:89).

Now the Bible does not fear investigation. Instead of fearing it, the Bible courts and challenges consideration and examination. The more widely it is known, the more closely it is read, the more carefully it is studied, the more unreservedly will it be received as the Word of God. Christians are not a company of enthusiastic fanatics. They are not lovers of myths. They are not anxious to believe a delusion. They do not desire their lives to be molded by an empty superstition. They do not wish to mistake hallucination for inspiration. If they are wrong, they wish to be set right. If they are deceived, they want to be disillusioned. If they are mistaken, they desire to be corrected.

The first question which the thoughtful reader of the Bible has to answer is, What importance and value am I to attach to the contents of the Scriptures? Were the writers of the Bible so many fanatics moved by oracular frenzy? Were they merely poetically inspired and intellectually elevated? Or were they, as they claimed to be, and as the Scriptures affirm they were, moved by the Holy Spirit to act as the voice of God to a sinful world? Were the writers of the Bible inspired by God in a manner no other men were in any other age of the world? Were they invested and endowed with the power to disclose mysteries and point men upward and onward to that which otherwise would have been an impenetrable future? One can readily appreciate the fact that the answer to these questions is of supreme importance. If the Bible is not inspired in the strictest sense of the word then it is worthless, for it claims to be God's Word, and if its claims are spurious, then its statements are unreliable and its contents are untrustworthy. If, on the other hand, it can be shown to the satisfaction of every impartial inquirer that the Bible is the Word of God, inerrant and infallible, then we have a starting point from which we can advance to the conquest of all truth.

A book that claims to be a *Divine revelation*—a claim

which, as we shall see, is substantiated by the most convincing credentials—cannot be rejected or even neglected without grave peril to the soul. True wisdom cannot refuse to examine it with care and impartiality. If the claims of the Bible be well founded, then the prayerful and diligent study of the Scriptures becomes of paramount importance: they have a claim upon our notice and time which nothing else has, and beside them everything in this world loses its luster and sinks into utter insignificance. If the Bible is the *Word of God*, then it infinitely transcends in value all the writings of men, and in exact ratio to its immeasurable superiority to human productions, such is our responsibility and duty to give it the most reverent and serious consideration. As a Divine revelation, the Bible ought to be studied, yet this is the only subject on which human curiosity does not desire information. Into every other sphere man pushes his investigations, but the Book of books is neglected, and this, not only by the ignorant, and illiterate, but by the wise of this world as well. The cultured dilettante will boast of his acquaintance with the sages of Greece and Rome, yet will know little or nothing of Moses and the prophets, Christ and His Apostles. But the general neglect of the Bible verifies the Scriptures and affords an additional proof of their authenticity. The contempt with which the Bible is treated demonstrates that human nature is exactly what God's Word represents it to be—fallen and depraved—and is unmistakable evidence that the carnal mind is enmity against God.

If the Bible is the Word of God; if it stands on an infinitely exalted plane, all alone; if it immeasurably transcends all the greatest productions of human genius; then, we should naturally expect to find that it has unique credentials, that there are internal marks which prove it to be the handiwork of God, that there is conclusive evidence to show that its Author is the supreme being, Divine. That these expectations are realized, we shall now endeavor to show; that there is no reason, whatever, for anyone to doubt the Divine inspiration of the Scriptures is the purpose of this book to demonstrate. As we examine the natural world, we find innumerable proofs of the existence of a Personal Creator, and the same God who has manifested Himself through His works has also revealed His wisdom and will through His Word. The God of creation and the God of written revelation are One, and there are irrefutable arguments to show that the Almighty who made the heavens and the earth is also the Author of the Bible.

We shall now submit to the critical attention of the reader a few of the lines of demonstration which argue for the Divine inspiration of the Bible.

1. There Is a Presumption in Favor of the Bible

This argument may be simply and tersely stated thus—Man needed a Divine revelation couched in human language. God had previously given man a revelation of Himself in His created works—which men please to term *nature*—but bears unmistakable testimony to the existence of its Creator, and though sufficient is revealed of God through it to render all men *"without excuse,"* (Romans 1:20) yet creation does not present a complete unveiling of God's character. Creation reveals God's wisdom and power, but it gives us a very imperfect presentation of His mercy and love. Creation is now under the curse; it is imperfect, because it has been marred by sin; therefore, an imperfect creation cannot be a perfect medium for revealing God; and hence also, the testimony of creation is *contradictory*.

In the year's spring, when nature puts on her loveliest robes and we see the beautiful foliage of the countryside and listen to the joyful songs of the birds, we have no difficulty in inferring that a gracious God is ruling over our world. But what of the wintertime, when the countryside is desolate and the trees are leafless and forlorn, when a pall of death seems to rest on everything? When we stood by the seashore and watched the setting sun crimsoning the placid waters on a quiet eve, we had no hesitation in ascribing the picture to the hand of the Divine Artist. But when we stand upon the same seashore on a stormy night, hear the roaring of the breakers and the howling wind, see the boats battling with the angry waves and listen to the heart-rending cries of the sailors as they go down into a watery grave we are tempted to wonder if a merciful God is at the helm. As one walks through the Grand Canyon or stands before the Niagara Falls, the hand and power of God seem very evident; but, as one witnesses the desolations of the San Francisco earthquake or the death-dealing effects of the volcanic eruptions of Mount Vesuvius, he is again perplexed and puzzled. In a word, then, the testimony of nature is conflicting, and, as we have said, this is because sin has come in and marred God's handiwork. Creation displays God's *natural* attributes, but it tells us little or nothing of His *moral* perfections. Nature knows no forgiveness and shows no mercy, and if we had no other source of information, we should never discover the fact that God pardons sinners. Man *needs* a written revelation from God.

Our limitations and our ignorance reveal our need. Man is in darkness concerning *God*. Blot the Bible out of existence and what should we know about His character, His moral attributes, His attitude toward us, or His demands upon us? As we have seen, nature is but an imperfect medium for revealing God. The ancients had the same nature before them as we have, but what did they discover of His character? Unto what knowledge of the one true God did they attain? The seventeenth chapter of the Acts answers that question. When the Apostle Paul was in the famous city of Athens, famous for its learning and philosophical culture, he discovered an altar, on which were inscribed the words,

"To the *unknown God*". The same condition prevails today. Visit those lands which have not been illumined by the light of the Holy Scriptures and it will be found that their peoples know no more about the character of the living God than did the ancient Egyptians and Babylonians.

Man is in darkness concerning *himself*. From whence am I? What am I? Am I anything more than a reasoning animal? Have I an immortal soul, or, am I nothing more than a sentient being? What is the purpose of my existence? Why am I here in this world at all? What is the end and aim of life? How shall I employ my time and talents? Shall I live only for today, eat, drink, and be merry? What after death? Do I perish like the beasts of the field, or is the grave the portal into another world? If so, whither am I bound? Do these questions appear senseless and irrelevant? Annihilate the Scriptures, eliminate all the light they have shed upon these problems, and whither shall we turn for a solution? If the Bible had never been written how many of these questions could have been satisfactorily answered? A very striking testimony to man's need of a Divine revelation was given by the celebrated but skeptical historian Gibbon. He remarked—"Since, therefore, the most sublime efforts of philosophy can extend no farther than feebly to point out the desire, the hope, or, at most, the probability, of a future state, *there is nothing except a Divine revelation* that can ascertan the existence and describe the condition of the invisible country which is destine to receive the souls of men after their separation from the body."

Our *experiences* reveal our need. There are problems to be faced which our wisdom is incapable of solving; there are obstacles in our path which we have no means of surmounting; there are enemies to be met which we are unable to vanquish. We are in dire need of counsel, strength, and courage. There are trials and tribulations which come to us, testing the hearts of the bravest and stoutest, and we need comfort and cheer. There are sorrows and bereavements which crush our spirits and we need the hope of immortality and resurrection.

Our *corporate life* reveals our need. What is to govern and regulate our dealings one with the other? Shall each do that which is right in his own eyes? That would destroy all law and order. Shall we draw up some moral code, some ethical standard? But who shall fix it? Opinions vary. We need some final court of appeal: if we had no Bible, where should we find it?

Man then *needs a* Divine revelation; God is *able* to supply that need; therefore, is it not *reasonable* to suppose He will do so? Surely God will not mock our ignorance and leave us to grope in the dark! If it is harder to believe that the universe had no creator, than it is to believe that "in the beginning God created the heavens and the earth;" if it is a greater tax upon our faith to suppose that Christianity with all its glorious triumphs is without a Divine Founder, than it is to believe that it rests upon the Person of the Lord Jesus Christ; then, does it not also make a greater demand upon human credulity to imagine that God would leave mankind without an intelligible communication from Himself, than it does to believe that the Bible is a revelation from the Creator to His fallen and erring creatures?

If there is a personal God (and none but a "fool" will deny His existence), and if we are the works of His hands, He surely would not leave us in doubt concerning the great problems which have to do with our temporal, spiritual, and eternal welfare. If an earthly parent advises his sons and daughters on their problems and perplexities, warns them of the perils and pitfalls of life which menace their well-being; counsels them with regard to their daily welfare and makes known to them his plans and purposes concerning their future. Surely it is incredible to suppose that our Heavenly Father would do less for His children!

We are often uncertain as to which is the right course to pursue; we are frequently in doubt as to the real path of duty; we are constantly surrounded by the hosts of wickedness which seek to accomplish our downfall; and, we are daily confronted with experiences which make us sad and sorrowful. The wisest among us need guidance which our own wisdom fails to supply; the best of humanity need grace which the human heart is powerless to bestow; the most refined among the sons of men need deliverance from temptations which they cannot overcome. Will God mock us then in our need? Will God leave us alone in the hour of our weakness? Will God refuse to provide for us a Refuge from our enemies? Man needs a Counselor, a Comforter, a Deliverer. The very fact that God has a Father's regard for His children necessitates that He should give them a written revelation which communicates His mind and will concerning them and which points them to the One who is willing and able to supply all their need.

To sum up this argument. Man *needs* a Divine revelation; God is *able* to supply one; is it not, therefore, *reasonable* to suppose He will do so? There is then, a presumption in favor of the Bible. Is it not more reasonable to believe that He whose name and nature is Love shall provide us with a lamp unto our feet and a light unto our path, than to leave us to grope our way amid the darkness of a fallen and ruined world?

2. The Perennial Freshness of the Bible Bears Witness to its Divine Inspirer

The full force of the present argument will appeal only to those who are intimately acquainted with the Bible, and the more familiar the reader is with the Sacred Canon the more heartily will he endorse the following statements. Just as a knowledge of Latin is necessary in order to understand the technique of a treatise on pathology or physiology, or just as a certain amount of culture and academic learning is an indispensable adjunct to follow intelligently the arguments and apprehend the illustrations in a dissertation on philosophy or psychology, so a first-hand acquaintance with the Bible is necessary to appreciate the fact that its contents never become commonplace.

One of the first facts which arrests the attention of the student of God's Word is that, like the widow's oil and meal which nourished Elijah, the contents of the Bible are never exhausted. Unlike all other books, the Bible never acquires a sameness, and never diminishes in its power of response to the needy soul which comes to it. Just as a fresh supply of manna was given each day to the Israelites in the wilderness, so the Spirit of God ever breaks anew the Bread of Life to them who hunger after righteousness; or, just as the loaves and fishes in the hands of our Lord were more than enough to feed the famished multitude—a surplus still remaining—so the honey and milk of the Word are more than sufficient to satisfy the hunger of every human soul—the supply still remaining undiminished for new generations.

Although one may know, word for word, the entire contents of some chapter of Scripture, and although he may have taken the time to ponder thoughtfully every sentence therein, yet, on every subsequent occasion, provided one comes to it again in the spirit of humble inquiry, each fresh reading will reveal new gems never seen there before and new delights will be experienced never met with previously. The most familiar passages will yield as much refreshment at the thousandth perusal as they did at the first. The Bible has been likened to a fountain of living water: the fountain is ever the same, but the water is always fresh.

Herein, the Bible differs from all other books, sacred or secular. What man has to say can be gathered from his writings at the first reading: failure to do so indicates that the writer has not succeeded in expressing himself clearly, or else the reader has failed to apprehend his meaning. Man is only able to deal with surface things, hence he cares only about surface appearances; consequently, whatever man has to say lies upon the surface of his writings, and the capable reader can exhaust them by a single perusal. Not so with the Bible. Although the Bible has been studied more microscopically than any other book (even its very letters have been counted and registered) by many of the keenest intellects for the past two thousand years, although whole libraries of works have been written as commentaries upon its teachings, and although literally millions of sermons have been preached and printed in the attempt to expound every part of Holy Writ, yet its contents have not been exhausted, and in this twentieth century new discoveries are being made in it every day!

The Bible is an inexhaustible mine of wealth: it is the El Dorado of heavenly treasure. It has veins of ore which never "give out" and pockets of gold which no pick can empty; yet, like earthly treasures, the gems of God must be diligently sought if they are to be found. Potatoes lie near the surface of the ground, but diamonds require much laborious digging, so also the precious things of the Word are only revealed to the prayerful, patient and diligent student.

The Bible is like a spring of water which never runs dry. No matter how many may drink from its life-giving stream, and no matter how often they may quench their thirst at its refreshing waters, its flow continues and never fails to satisfy the needs of all who come and take of its perennial springs. The Bible has a whole continent of Truth yet to be explored. A learned scholar who died during the present year of grace had read through the Bible no fewer than five hundred times! What other book, ancient or modern, Oriental or Occidental, would repay even a fiftieth reading?

How can we account for this marvelous characteristic of the Bible? What explanation can we offer for this startling phenomenon? It is only stating a commonplace axiom when we affirm that what is finite is fathomable. What the mind of man has produced, the mind of man can exhaust. If human mortals had written the Bible, its contents would have been "mastered" ages ago. In view of the fact that the contents of the Scriptures cannot be exhausted, that they never acquire sameness or staleness to the devout student, and that they always speak with fresh force to the quickened soul that comes to them, is it not apparent that none other than the infinite mind of God could have created such a wonderful Book as the Bible?

3. The Unmistakable Honesty of the Writers of the Bible Attests to its Heavenly Origin

The title of this chapter suggests a wide field of study the limits of which we can now only skirt here and there. To begin with the writers of the Old Testament.

Had the historical parts of the Old Testament been a forgery, or the production of uninspired men, their contents would have been very different to what they are. Each of its Books was written by a descendant of Abraham, yet nowhere do we find the bravery of the Israelites extolled and never once are their victories regarded as the outcome of their courage or military genius; on the contrary, success is attributed to the presence of Jehovah the God of Israel. To this it might be replied, Heathen writers have often ascribed the victories of their peoples to the intervention of their gods. This is true, yet there is no parallel at all between the two cases. Comparison is impossible. Heathen writers invariably represent their gods as being blindly partial to their friends and whenever their favorites failed to come out victorious their defeat is attributed to the opposition of other gods or to a blind and unyielding fate. In contradistinction to this, the *defeats* of Israel, as much as their victories, are regarded as coming from Jehovah. Their successes were not due to mere *partiality* in God, but are uniformly viewed as connected with a careful observance of His commands; and, in like manner, their defeats are portrayed as the outcome of their disobedience and waywardness. If they transgressed His laws they were defeated and put to shame, even though their God was the Almighty. But we have digressed somewhat. That to which we desire to direct attention is the fact that men who were *their own countrymen* have chronicled the history of the Israelites, and therein have faithfully recorded their defeats not to an inexorable fate, nor to bad generalship and military failures, but to the sins of the people and their wickedness against God. Such a God is not the creation of the human mind, and such historians were not actuated by the common principles of human nature.

Not only have the Jewish historians recounted the military defeats of their people, but they have also faithfully recorded their many moral backslidings and spiritual declinations. One of the outstanding truths of the Old Testament is that the Unity of God, that God is One, that beside Him there is none else, that all other gods are false gods and that to pay them homage is to be guilty of the sin of idolatry. Against the sin of idolatry these Jewish writers cry out repeatedly. They uniformly declare that it is a sin most abhorrent in the sight of heaven. Yet, these same Jewish writers record how again and again their ancestors (contrary to the universal leaning towards ancestral adoration and worship), and their contemporaries, were guilty of this great wickedness. Not only so, but they have pointed out how some of their most famous heroes sinned in this very particular. Aaron and the golden calf, Solomon and the later kings being notable examples—"*Then did Solomon build a high place for Chemosh, the abomination of Moab, in the hill that is before Jerusalem, and for Molech, the abomination of the children of Ammon. And likewise did he for all his strange wives, which burnt incense and sacrificed unto their gods*" (1 Kings 11:7-8). Moreover, there is no attempt made to excuse their wrongdoing; instead, their acts are openly censured and uncompromisingly condemned. As is well known, human historians are inclined to conceal or extenuate the faults of their favorites. A forged history would have clothed friends with every virtue, and would not have ventured to mar the effect designed to be produced by uncovering the vices of its most distinguished personages. Here, then, is displayed the *uniqueness* of Scripture history. Its characters are painted in the colors of truth and nature. But such characters were never sketched by a human pencil. Moses and the other writers must have written by Divine inspiration.

The sin of idolatry, while it is the worst of which Israel was guilty, is not the only evil recorded against them—their whole history is one long story of repeated apostasy from Jehovah their God. After they had been emancipated from the bondage of Egypt and had been miraculously delivered from their cruel masters at the Red Sea, they commenced their journey towards the Promised Land. Between them and their goal lay a march across the wilderness, and here the depravity of their hearts was fully manifested. In spite of the fact that Jehovah, by overthrowing their enemies, had plainly demonstrated that He was their God, yet no sooner was the faith of the Israelites put to the test than their hearts failed them. First, their stores of food began to give out and they feared they would perish from hunger. Trying circumstances had banished the Living God from their thoughts. They complained of their lot and murmured against Moses. Yet God did not deal with them after their sins nor reward them according to their iniquities: in mercy, He gave them bread from heaven and furnished them a daily supply of manna. But they soon became dissatisfied with the manna and lusted after the flesh pots of Egypt. Still God dealt with them in grace.

Shortly after God's intervention in giving the Israelites food to eat, which ought for ever to have closed their murmuring mouths, they pitched in Rephidim where "*there was no water for the people to drink. Wherefore the people did chide with Moses, and said, Give us water that we may drink. And Moses said unto them, Why chide ye with me? wherefore do ye tempt the Lord? And the people thirsted there for water; and the people murmured against Moses, and said, Wherefore is this that thou hast brought us up out of Egypt, to kill us and our children and our cattle with thirst? And Moses cried unto the Lord, saying, What shall I do unto this people? they be almost ready to stone me.*" What was God's response? Did His anger consume them? Did He refuse to bear longer with such a stiff-necked people? No: "*The Lord said unto Moses, Go on before the people, and take with thee of the elders of Israel; and thy rod, wherewith thou smotest the river, take in thine hand, and go. Behold, I will stand before thee there upon the rock in Horeb; and thou shalt smite the rock, and there shall come water out of it, that the people may drink*" (Exodus 17:1-7).

The above incidents were but sadly typical and illustrative of Israel's general conduct. When the spies were sent out to view the Promised Land and returned and reported, ten of them magnified the difficulties which confronted them and advised the people not to attempt an occupation of Canaan; and though the remaining two faithfully reminded the Israelites that the mighty Jehovah could easily overcome all their difficulties, nevertheless, the nation listened not but heeded the word of their skeptical advisers. Time after time they provoked Jehovah, and in consequence the whole of that generation perished in the wilderness. When the succeeding generation was grown, under the leadership of Joshua they entered the Promised Land and by the aid of God overthrew many of their enemies and occupied much of their territory. But after the death of Joshua we read, "There arose another generation after them, which knew not the Lord, nor yet the works which He had done for Israel. And the children of Israel did evil in the sight of the Lord God of their fathers, which brought them out of the land of Egypt, and followed other gods, of the gods of the people that were round about them, and bowed themselves unto them, and provoked the Lord to anger. And they forsook the Lord, and served Baal and Ashtaroth" (Judges 2:10-13). There is no need for us to follow further the fluctuating fortunes of Israel: as is well known, under the period of the judges their history was a series of returns to the Lord and subsequent departures from Him; repeated deliverances from the hands of their enemies, and then returning unfaithfulness on their part, followed by being again delivered unto their foes. Under the kings it was no better. The very first of their kings perished through his willful disobedience and apostasy; the third king, Solomon, violated God's law and married heathen women who turned his heart unto false gods. Solomon, in turn, was followed by a number of idolatrous rulers, and the path of Israel ran farther and farther away from the Lord, until He delivered them over unto Nebuchadnezzar who captured their beloved Jerusalem, destroyed their Temple, and carried away the people into captivity.

In the repeated mention which we have in the Old Testament of Israel's sins, we discover, in light as clear as day, the absolute honesty and candor of those who recorded Israel's history. No attempt whatever is made to conceal their folly, their unbelief, and their wickedness; instead, the corrupt condition of their hearts is made fully manifest, and this, by writers who belonged to, and were born of the same nation. In the whole realm of literature, there is no parallel. The record of Israel's history is absolutely unique. The careful reader would at first conclude that Israel as a nation was more depraved than any other, yet further reflection will show that the inference is a false one and that the real fact is that the history of Israel has been *more faithfully transmitted* than that of any other nation. We mean the history of Israel as it is recorded in the Holy Scriptures, for in striking contrast thereto and in exemplification of all that we have written above, it is noteworthy that Josephus *passes over in silence* whatever appeared unfavorable to his nation!!

Coming now to the New Testament, we begin with the character of John the Baptist and the position that he occupied. John the Baptist is presented as a most eminent personage. We are told that his birth was due to the miraculous intervention of God. We learn that he was *"filled with the Holy Spirit, even from his mother's womb"* (Luke 1:15). John the Baptist was himself the subject of Old

Testament prediction. The office that he filled was the most honorable which ever fell to the lot of any member of Adam's race. He was the harbinger of the Messiah. He was the one who went before our Lord to prepare His way. He had the honor of baptizing the blessed Redeemer. Now where would human wisdom have placed him among the attendants of the Lord Jesus? What position would it have ascribed to him? Surely he would have been set forth as the most distinguished among our Lord's followers; surely, human wisdom would have set him at the right hand of the Savior! Yet what do we find? Instead of this, we discover that he had no familiar discourse with the Savior; instead, we find he was treated with apparent neglect; instead, we find him represented as occupying the position of a doubter who, as the result of his imprisonment, was constrained to send a message to his Master to enquire whether or not He were the promised Messiah. Had his character been the invention of forgery, nothing would have been heard of his lapse of faith. Indeed, this is so opposed to the dictates of human wisdom, that many have been shocked at the thought of ascribing doubts to the eminent forerunner of Christ, and have taxed their ingenuity to the utmost to force from the obvious meaning of the record some other and some different signification. But all these ingenuities of human sophistry are dissipated by the reply which our Lord made on the occasion of John's inquiry (Matthew 11:1-6), a reply which shows very plainly that the question was asked not for the benefit of his disciples, but because the Baptist's own heart was harassed with doubts. Again, we say that no human mind could have invented the character of John the Baptist, and the faithfulness of his biographers is another proof that the writers of the Bible were actuated by something more and something higher than the principles of human nature.

Another striking illustration of our chapter heading—one which many writers have pointed out—is the treatment the Son of God received while He tabernacled among men. For two thousand years Israel's hopes had all centered in the advent of their Messiah. The height of every Jewish woman's ambition was that she might be selected of God to have the honor of being the mother of the promised Seed. For centuries, every pious Hebrew had looked and longed for the day when He should appear who was to occupy David's throne and rule and reign in righteousness. Yet, when He did appear how was the Promised One received? *"He was despised and rejected of men"* (Isaiah 53:3) *"He came unto His own and His own received Him not"* (John 1:11). Those who were His brethren according to the flesh *"hated"* Him *"without a cause"* (John 15:25). The very nation which gave Him birth and to which He ministered in infinite grace and blessing demanded that He should be crucified. The startling thing which we desire to particularly emphasize is, that the narrators of this awful tragedy are fellow countrymen of those upon whose heads rested the guilt of its perpetration. It was Jewish writers who recorded the fearful crime of the Jewish nation against their Messiah! And, we say again, that in the recording of that crime, no attempt whatever is made to palliate or extenuate their wickedness; instead, it is denounced and condemned in the most uncompromising terms. Israel is openly charged with having taken and with "wicked hands...slain" the Lord of Glory (Acts 2:23). Such an honest and impartial recital of

Israel's crowning sin can only be explained on the ground that what these men wrote was inspired of God.

One more illustration must suffice. After our Lord's death and resurrection, He commissioned His disciples to go forth carrying from Him a message first to His own nation and later to *"every creature"* (Mark 16:15-16). This message, be it noted, was not a malediction called down upon the heads of His heartless murderers, but a proclamation of grace. It was a message of good news, of glad tidings—*forgiveness* was to be preached in His name to all men. How then would human wisdom suppose such a message will be received? It is further to be observed that those who were thus commissioned to carry the Gospel to the lost were vested with power to heal the sick and to cast out demons. Surely, such a beneficent ministry will meet with a universal welcome! Yet, incredible as it may appear, the Apostles of Christ met with no more appreciation than did their Master. They, too, were despised and rejected. They, too, were hated and persecuted. They, too, were ill-treated, imprisoned, and put to a shameful death. And this, not merely from the hands of the bigoted Jews, but from the cultured Greeks and from the democratic and freedom loving Romans as well. Though these Apostles brought blessing, they themselves were cursed; though they sought to emancipate men from the thralldom of sin and Satan, yet they were themselves captured and thrown into prison; though they healed the sick and raised the dead, they suffered martyrdom. Surely it is apparent to every impartial mind that the New Testament is no mere human invention; and surely it is evident from the honesty of its writers in so faithfully portraying the enmity of the carnal mind against God, that their productions can only be accounted for on the ground that they spake and wrote "*not of themselves,*" but "*as they were moved by the Holy Spirit*" (2 Peter 1:21).

4. The Character of its Teachings Evidences the Divine Authorship of the Bible

Take its teachings about *God Himself*. What does the Bible teach us about God? It declares that He is *Eternal*: "Before the mountains were brought forth, or ever Thou hadst formed the earth and the world, even from everlasting to everlasting, Thou are God" (Psalm 90:2). It reveals the fact that He is *Infinite*: "But will God indeed dwell on the earth? Behold, the heaven and heaven of heavens cannot contain Thee" (1 Kings 8:27). Vast as we know the universe to be, it has its bounds; but we must go beyond them to conceive of God—"Canst thou by searching find out God? Canst thou find out the Almighty unto perfection? It is as high as heaven; what canst thou do? deeper than hell; what canst thou know? The measure thereof is longer than the earth, and broader than the sea" (Job 11:7-9). It makes mention of His *Sovereignty*: "Remember the former things of old: for I am God, and there is none else; I am God, and there is none like Me, declaring the end from the beginning, and from ancient times the things that are not yet done, saying, My counsel shall stand, and I will do all My pleasure" (Isaiah 46:9-10). It affirms that He is *Omnipotent*: "Behold I am the Lord, the God of all flesh: is there anything too hard for Me?" (Jeremiah 32:27). It intimates that He is *Omniscient*: "*Great is our Lord, and of great power: His understanding is infinite*" (Psalm 147:5). It teaches that He is *Omnipresent*: "*Can any hide himself in secret places that I shall not see him? saith the Lord. Do not I fill heaven and earth? saith the Lord*" (Jeremiah 23:24). It declares that He is *Immutable*: "*The same yesterday, and today, and forever*" (Hebrews 13:8). Yea, that with Him "*is no variableness, neither shadow of turning*" (James 1:17). It reveals that He is "*The Judge of all the earth*" (Genesis 18:25) and that everyone shall yet have to "*give an account of himself to God*" (Romans 14:12). It announces that He is *inflexibly just* in all His dealings so that He can by "*no means clear the guilty*" (Numbers 14:18); that all will be judged "*according to their works*" (Revelation 20:12), and that they shall reap "*whatsoever*" they have sown (Galatians 6:7). It reveals the fact that He is *absolutely holy*, dwelling in light inaccessible. So holy that even the seraphim have to veil their faces in His presence (Isaiah 6:2). So holy that the heavens are not clean in His sight (Job 15:15). So holy that the best of men when face to face with their Maker, have to cry, "*I abhor myself*" (Job 42:6); "*Woe is me! For I am undone*" (Isaiah 6:5). Such a delineation of Deity is as far beyond man's conception as the heavens are above the earth. No man, and no number of men, ever invented such a God as this. Ransack the libraries of the ancient, examine the musings of the mystics, study the religions of the heathen and nothing will be found which can for a moment be compared with the sublime and exalted description of God's character which is furnished by the Bible.

The teachings of the Bible about man are unique. Unlike all other books in the world, the Bible condemns man and all his doings. It never eulogizes his wisdom, nor praises his achievements. On the contrary, it declares that *"every man at his best state is altogether vanity"* (Psalm 39:5). Instead of teaching that man is a noble character, evolving heavenwards, it tells him that all his righteousness (his best works) are as *"filthy rags"* (Isaiah 64:6), that he is a lost sinner, incapable of bettering his condition; that he is deserving only of Hell.

The picture which the Scriptures give of man is deeply humiliating and entirely different from all which are drawn by human pencils. The Word of God describes the state of the natural man in the following language:—*"There is none righteous, no, not one. There is none that understandeth, there is none that seeketh after God. They are all gone out of the way, they are together become unprofitable. There is none that doeth good, no, not one. Their throat is an open sepulcher; with their tongues they have used deceit; the poison of asps is under their lips; whose mouth is full of cursing and bitterness. Their feet are swift to shed blood: destruction and misery are in their ways: and the way of peace have they not known. There is no fear of God before their eyes"* (Romans 3:10-18).

Instead of making Satan the source of all the black crimes of which we are guilty, the Bible declares, *"For from within, out of the heart of man proceed evil thoughts, adulteries, fornications, murders, thefts, covetousness, wickedness, deceit, lasciviousness, an evil eye, blasphemy, pride, foolishness: all these evil things come from within and defile the man"* (Mark 7:21-23). Such a conception of man—so different from man's own ideas, and so humiliating to his proud heart—never could have emanated from man himself.

"*The heart is deceitful above all things and desperately wicked*" (Jeremiah 17:9) is a concept that never originated in any human mind.

The teachings of the Bible about *the world* are unique. In nothing perhaps are the teachings of Scripture and the writings of man at such variance as they are at this point. Using the term as meaning the world-system in contradistinction to the earth, what is the direction of man's thoughts concerning the same? Man thinks highly of the world, for he regards it as his world. It is that which his labors have produced and he looks upon it with satisfaction and pride. He boasts that "the world is growing better." He declares that the world is becoming more civilized and more humanized. Man's thoughts on this subject have been well summarized by the poet in the familiar language—"God is in heaven: All's well with the world." But what saith the Scriptures? Upon this subject, too, we discover that God's thoughts are very different from ours. The Bible uniformly *condemns* the world and speaks of it as a thing of evil. We shall not attempt to quote every passage which does this, but shall merely single out a few specimen Scriptures.

"*If the world hate you, ye know that it hated Me before it hated you. If ye were of the world, the world would love his own: but because ye are not of the world, but I have chosen you out of the world, therefore the world hateth you*" (John 15:18-19). This passage teaches that the world *hates* both Christ and His followers. "*The wisdom of this world is foolishness with God*" (I Corinthians 3:19). Certainly no uninspired pen wrote these words. "*Ye adulterers and adulteresses, know ye not that the friendship of the world is enmity with God? Whosoever therefore will be a friend of the world is the enemy of God"* (James 4:4). Here again, we learn that the world is an evil thing, condemned by God, and to be shunned by His children. *"Love not the world, neither the things that are in the world. If any man love the world, the love of the Father is not in him. For all that is in the world, the lust of the flesh, and the lust of the eyes, and the pride of life, is not of the Father, but is of the world"* (1 John 2:15-16). Here we have a *definition* of the world: it is all that is opposed to the Father—opposed in its principles and philosophy, its maxims and methods, its aims and ambitions, its trend and its end *"And the whole world lieth in the evil nne"* (I John 5:19, ASV). Here we learn why it is that the world hates Christ and His followers; why its wisdom is foolishness with God; why it is condemned by God and must be shunned by His children—it is under the dominion of that old serpent, the devil, whom Scripture specifically denominates *"The prince of this world"* (John 16:11).

The teachings of the Bible about sin is unique. Man regards sin as a misfortune and ever seeks to minimize its enormity. In these days, sin is referred to as ignorance, as a necessary stage in man's development. By others, sin is looked upon as a mere negation, the opposite of good; while Mrs. Eddy and her followers went so far as to deny its existence altogether. But the Bible, unlike every other book, strips man of all excuses and emphasizes his culpability. In the Bible, sin is never palliated or extenuated, but from first to last the Holy Scriptures insist upon its enormity and heinousness. The Word of God declares that *"sin is very grievous"* (Genesis 18:20) and that our sins provoke God to anger (1 Kings 16:2). It speaks of the *"deceitfulness of sin"* (Hebrews 3:13) and insists that sin is *"exceedingly sinful"* (Romans 7:13). It declares that all sin is sin against God (Psalm 51:4) and against His Christ (1 Corinthians 8:12). It regards our sins as being *"as scarlet"* and *"red like crimson"* (Isaiah 1:18). It declares that sin is more than an act, it is an attitude. It affirms that sin is more than a non-compliance with God's law—it is rebellion against the One who gave the law . It teaches that *"sin is lawlessness"* (1 John 3:4, ASV), which means that sin is spiritual anarchy, open defiance against the Almighty. Moreover, it singles out no particular class; it condemns all alike. It announces that *"all have sinned and come short of the glory of God,"* that *"there is none righteous, no, not one"* (Romans 3:9, 23). Did man ever write such an indictment against himself? What human mind ever invented such a description of sin as that discovered in the Bible? Whoever would have imagined that sin was such a vile and dreadful thing in the sight of God that nothing but the precious blood of His own beloved Son could make an atonement for it!

The teaching of the Bible about *the punishment of sin* is unique. A defective view of sin necessarily leads to an inadequate conception of what is due sin. Minimize the gravity and enormity of sin and you must proportionately reduce the sentence which it deserves. Many are crying out today against the justice of the eternal punishment of sin. They complain that the penalty does not fit the crime. They argue that it is unrighteous for a sinner to suffer eternally in consequence of a short life span of wrong doing. But even in this world it is not the length of time which it takes to commit the crime which determines the severity of the sentence. Many a man has suffered a life term of imprisonment for a crime which required only a few minutes for its perpetration. Apart, however, from this consideration, *eternal* punishment is just if sin be looked at from *God's* viewpoint. But this is just what the majority of men refuse to do. They look at sin and its deserts solely from the human side. One reason why the Bible was written was to correct our ideas and views about sin, to teach us what an unspeakably awful and vile thing it is, to show us sin as God sees it. For one single sin Adam and Eve were banished from Eden. For one single sin Canaan and all his posterity were cursed. For a single sin Korah and his company went down alive into the pit. For one single sin Moses was debarred from entering the Promised Land. For a single sin Achan and his family were stoned to death. For a single sin Elisha's servant was smitten with leprosy. For a single sin Ananias and Sapphira were cut off out of the land of the living. Why? To teach us what an infinite evil it is to revolt against the thrice holy God. We repeat, that did men but see the terribleness of sin—did they but see that it was sin that put to a shameful death the Lord of Glory—then they would realize that nothing short of *eternal punishment* would meet the demands which justice has upon sinners.

But the great majority of men do not see the rightness or justice of eternal punishment; on the contrary, they cry out against it. In lands which were not illumined by the Old Testament Scriptures, where there existed any belief in a future life, it was held that at death the wicked either passed through some temporary suffering for remedial and purifying purposes or else they were annihilated. Even in Christendom, where the Word of God has held a prominent and public place for centuries, the great bulk of the people do not believe in eternal punishment. They argue that God is too merciful and kind to ban one of His own creatures to endless misery. Yea, not a few of the Lord's own people are afraid to take the solemn teachings of the Scriptures on this subject at their face value. It is therefore evident that had the Bible been written by uninspired men; had it been a mere human composition, it certainly would *not* have taught the eternal and conscious torment of all who die out of Christ. The fact that the Bible *does* so teach is conclusive proof that it was written by men who spake not of themselves, but as they were "moved by the Holy Spirit."

The teachings of God's Word upon eternal punishment are as clear and explicit as they are solemn and awful. They declare that the doom of the Christ rejector is a conscious, never-ending, indescribable torment. The Bible depicts the place of punishment as a realm where the *"worm dieth not"* and *"the fire is not quenched"* (Mark 9:48). It speaks of it as a lake of fire and brimstone (Revelvation 20:10), where even a drop of water is denied the agonized sufferer (Luke 16:24). It declares that *"the smoke of their torment ascendeth up for ever and ever: and they have no rest day nor night"* (Revelation 14:11). It represents the world of the lost as a scene into which penetrates no light—*"the blackness of darkness forever"* (Jude 1:13)—a doom alleviated by no ray of hope. In short, the portion of the lost will be unbearable, yet it will have to be borne, and borne for ever. What mortal mind conceived of such a fate? Such a conception is too repugnant and repulsive to the human heart to have had its birth on the earth.

The teachings of the Bible about *Salvation from Sin* is

unique. Man's thoughts about salvation, like every other subject which engages his mind are defective and deficient. Hence the force of the admonition—"*Let the wicked forsake his way and the unrighteous man his thoughts*" (Isaiah 55:7). In the first place, left to himself, man fails to realize his need of salvation. In the pride of his heart he imagines that he is sufficient in himself, and through the darkening of his understanding by sin he fails to comprehend his ruined and lost condition. Like the self-righteous Pharisee, he thanks God that he is not as other men, that he is morally the superior of the savage or the criminal, and refuses to believe that so far as his standing before God is concerned there is *"no difference."* It is not until the Holy Spirit deals with him that man is constrained to cry, "*God be merciful to me a sinner*" (Luke 18:9-14).

In the second place, man is ignorant of *the way* of salvation. Even when man has been brought to the place where he recognizes that he is not prepared to meet God, and that if he died in his present state, he would be eternally lost; even then he has no right conception of the remedy. Being ignorant of God's righteousness, he goes about to establish his own righteousness. He supposes that he must make some personal reparation for his past wrongdoings, that he must work for his salvation, do something to merit the esteem of God, and thus win heaven as a reward. The highest concept of man's mind is that of *merit*. To him salvation is a wage to be earned, a crown to be coveted, a prize to be won. The proof of this is to be seen in the fact that even when pardon and life are presented as *a free gift*, the universal tendency, at first, is to regard it as being "too good to be true." Yet, such is the plain teaching of God's

Word—"*For by grace are ye saved through faith; and that not of yourselves: it is the gift of God: not of works; lest any man should boast*" (Ephesians 2:8–9). And again—"*Not by works of righteousness which we have done, but according to His mercy He saved us*" (Titus 3:5).

If it is true that man left to himself would never have fully realized his need of salvation, and would never have discovered that it was by grace through faith and not of works, how much less would the human mind have been capable of rising to the level of what God's Word teaches about the *nature* of salvation and the glorious and marvelous *destiny of the saved!* Who would have thought that the Maker and Ruler of the universe should lay hold of poor, fallen, depraved men and women and lifting them out of the miry clay should make them His own sons and daughters, and should seat them at His own table! Who would ever have suggested that those who deserve naught but everlasting shame and contempt should be made "heirs of God and joint-heirs with Christ"! Who would have dreamed that beggars should be lifted from the dunghill of sin and made to sit together with Christ in heavenly places! Who would have imagined that the corrupted offspring of disobedient Adam should be exalted to a position higher than that occupied by the unfallen angels! Who would have dared to affirm that one day we shall be "made like Christ" and "be for ever with the Lord"! Such concepts were as far beyond the reach of the highest human intellect as they were of the rudest savage. "*But as it is written, eye hath not seen, nor ear heard, neither have entered into the heart of man, the things which God hath prepared for them that love Him. But God hath revealed them unto us by His Spirit: for the Spirit searcheth all things, yea, the deep things of God"* (1 Corinthians 2:9-10).

Again we ask, what human intellect could have devised a means whereby God could be just and yet merciful, merciful and yet just? What mortal mind would ever have dreamed of a free and full salvation, bestowed on hell-deserving sinners, "without money and without price"! And what flight of carnal imagination would ever have conceived of the Son of God Himself being *"made...sin"*[1] (2 Corinthians 5:21) for us and dying the Just for the unjust?

The teaching of the Bible concerning the *Savior of sinners* is unique. The description which the Scriptures furnish of the Person, the Character, and the Work of the Lord Jesus Christ is without anything that approaches a parallel in the whole realm of literature. It is easier to suppose that man could create a world than to believe he invented the character of our adorable Redeemer. Given a piece of machinery that is delicate, complex, exact in all its movements, and we know it must be the product of a competent mechanic. Given a work of art that is beautiful, symmetrical, original, and we know it must be the product of a master artist. None but an Angelo could have designed Saint Peter's; none but a Raphael could have painted the "transfiguration;" none but a Milton could have written a "Paradise Lost." And, none but the Holy Spirit could have produced the peerless portrait of the Lord Jesus which we find in the Gospels. In Christ *all excellencies* combine. Here is one of the many respects in which He differs from all other Bible characters. In each of the great heroes of Scripture some trait stands out with peculiar distinctness—Noah, faithful testimony; Abraham, faith in

God; Isaac, submission to his father; Joseph, love for his brethren; Moses, unselfishness and meekness; Joshua, courage and leadership; Job, fortitude and patience; Daniel, fidelity to God; Paul, zeal in service; John, spiritual discernment—but in the Lord Jesus *every grace* is found. Moreover, in Him all these perfections were properly poised and balanced. He was meek yet regal; He was gentle yet fearless; He was compassionate yet just; He was submissive yet authoritative; He was Divine yet human; add to these, the fact that He was absolutely "without sin" and His uniqueness becomes apparent. Nowhere in all the writings of antiquity is there to be found the presentation of such a peerless and wondrous character.

Not only is the portrayal of Christ's *character* without any rival, but the teaching of the Bible concerning His Person and Work is also utterly incredible on any other basis save that they are part of a Divine *revelation*. Who would have dared to imagine the Creator and Upholder of the universe taking upon Himself the form of a servant and being made in the likeness of men? Who would have conceived the idea of the Lord of Glory being born in a manger? Who would have dreamed of the Object of angelic worship becoming so poor that he had not where to lay His head? Who would have declared that the One before whom the seraphim veil their faces should be led as a lamb to the slaughter, should have suffered His own blessed face to be defiled with the vile spittle of man, and should permit the creatures of His hand to scourge and buffet Him? Whoever would have conceived of Emmanuel becoming obedient unto death, even the death of the Cross!

Here then is an argument which the simplest can grasp.

The Scriptures contain their own evidence that they *are* Divinely inspired. Every page of Holy Writ is stamped with Jehovah's autograph. The uniqueness of its teachings demonstrates the uniqueness of its Source. The teachings of the Scriptures about God Himself, about man, about the world, about sin, about eternal punishment, about salvation, about the Lord Jesus Christ, are proof that the Bible is not the product of any man or any number of men, but is in truth a revelation from God.

Notes

1. "Sin" in this verse means sin offering.

5. The Fulfilled Prophecies of the Bible Bespeak the Omniscience of its Author

In Isaiah 41:21-23 we have what is probably the most remarkable challenge to be found in the Bible. *"Produce your cause, saith the Lord; bring forth your strong reasons, saith the King of Jacob. Let them bring them forth, and show us what shall happen; let them show the former things, what they be, that we may consider them, and know the latter end of them; or declare us things for to come. Show the things that are to come hereafter, that we may know that ye are gods."* This Scripture has both a negative and a positive value: negatively it suggests an infallible criterion by which we may test the claims of religious impostors; positively, it calls attention to an unanswerable argument for the truthfulness of God's Word. Jehovah bids the prophets of false faiths to predict successfully events lying in the far distant future and their success or failure will show whether or not they are gods or merely pretenders and deceivers. On the other hand, the demonstrated fact that God alone grasps the ages and in His Word declares the end from the beginning, shows that he *is* God and that Scriptures are His Inspired Revelation to mankind.

Again and again men have attempted to predict future events, but always with the most disastrous failure, the anticipations of the most far-seeing and the precautions of the wisest are mocked repeatedly by the bitter irony of events. Man stands before an impenetrable wall of darkness, he is unable to foresee the events of even the next hour. None knows what a day may bring forth. To the finite mind, the future is filled with unknown possibilities. How then can we explain the hundreds of detailed prophecies in the Scriptures which have been literally fulfilled to the letter, hundreds of years after they were uttered? How can we account for the fact that the Bible successfully foretold hundreds, and in some instances thousands of years beforehand, the History of the Jews, the Course of the Gentiles, and the Experiences of the Church? The most conservative of critics, and the most daring assailants of God's Word are compelled to acknowledge that all the Books of the Old Testament were written *hundreds of years before the incarnation of our Lord*, hence, the actual and accurate fulfillment of these prophecies can only be explained on the hypothesis that "*For the prophecy came not in old time by the will of man: but holy men of God spake as they were moved by the Holy Ghost*" (2 Peter 1:21).

The Inspirer of the Scriptures has told us that "*We have also a more sure word of prophecy; where unto ye do well that ye take heed as unto a light that shineth in a dark place*" (2 Peter 1:19). In the limited space at our command we shall appeal to but a few from among the many fulfilled prophecies of God's Word, and shall limit ourselves to those which have reference to *the Person and Work of the Lord Jesus Christ*. The cumulative force of these will be sufficient, we trust, to convince any impartial inquirer that none other but the mind of God could have disclosed the future and unveiled beforehand far distant events.

The testimony of Jesus is the *"spirit of prophecy"* (Revelation 19:10). The Lamb of God is the one great object and subject of the Prophetic Word. In Genesis 3:15 we have the first word about the Coming of Christ. Speaking to the serpent, Jehovah said, *"And I will put enmity between thee and the woman, and between thy seed and her seed; it shall bruise thy head, and thou shall bruise His heel."* Note that the Coming One was to be the *"woman's seed,"* the Miraculous Character of our Lord's Birth being thus foretold four thousand years before He was born at Bethlehem!

In Genesis 22:18, we have the second distinct Messianic prophecy. Unto Abraham, the angel of the Lord declared, *"And in thy seed shall all the nations of the earth be blessed."* Not only was the Savior of sinners to be human as well as Divine, not only was He to be the *"woman's"* seed, but in the above Scripture it was declared that He should be a descendant of Abraham—an Israelite. How this was fulfilled we may see by a reference to the first verse in the New Testament, where we are told (Matthew 1:1) that Jesus Christ was *"The Son of David, the son of Abraham."*

But still further was the compass narrowed down, for we have intimated in the Old Testament Scriptures the very *tribe* from which the Messiah was to issue—our Lord was to come of the tribe of *Judah*, the "kingly" tribe. He was to be a descendant of David. Nathan the prophet was commanded by God to go and say to David, *"I will set up thy* seed after thee, which shall proceed out of thy bowels, and I will stablish His kingdom. He shall build an house for My name, and I will stablish the throne of His kingdom forever" (2 Samuel 7:12-13). And again, in Psalm 132:11 David declares concerning the promised Messiah, "The Lord hath sworn in truth unto David; He will not turn from it; Of the fruit of thy body will I set upon thy throne."

Not only was our Lord's *nationality* defined hundreds of years before His incarnation, but the very *place* of His birth was also given. In Micah 5:2 we are informed, "But thou, Bethlehem Ephratah, though thou be little among the thousands of Judah, but out of thee shall He come forth unto Me that is to be Ruler in Israel; whose goings forth have been from of old, from the days of eternity." Christ was to be born in Bethlehem, and not only in one of the several villages which bore that name in Palestine, but Bethlehem of Judea was to be the birth-place of the world's Redeemer; and though Mary was a native of Nazareth, far distant from Bethlehem, yet through the providence of God, His Word was literally fulfilled by His Son being born in Bethlehem of Judea.

Further, the very *time* of Messiah's appearing was given through both Jacob and Daniel (see Genesis 49:10 and Daniel 9:24-26). Now in order to appreciate the force of these marvelous, super-natural prophecies, let the reader seek to foretell the nationality, place and time of the birth of someone who shall be born in the twenty-fifth century AD, and then he will realize that none but a man inspired and informed by God Himself could perform such an otherwise impossible feat.

So definite and distinct were the Old Testament

The Divine Inspiration of the Bible | 43

prophecies respecting the Birth of Christ, that the hope of Israel became the Messianic Hope; all their expectations were centered in the coming of the Messiah. It is therefore the more remarkable that their sacred Scriptures should contain another set of prophecies which predicted that He should be despised by His own nation and rejected by His own kinsmen. We can only now call attention to one of the prophecies which declared that the Messiah of Israel should be slighted and scorned by His brethren according to the flesh.

In Isaiah 53:2-3 we read, "*And when we [Israel] shall see Him, there is no beauty that we should desire Him. He is despised and rejected of men; a Man of sorrows, and acquainted with grief; and we hid as it were our faces from Him; He was despised, and we esteemed Him not!*" We pause here for a moment to enlarge upon this strange and striking phenomenon.

For more than fifteen centuries, the Coming of the Messiah had been the one great national Hope of Israel. From the cradle, the sons of Abraham were taught to pray and long for His advent. The eagerness with which they awaited the appearing of the Star of Jacob is absolutely without parallel in the history of any other nation. How then can we account for the fact that when He did come He was despised and rejected? How can we explain the fact that side by side with the intense longing for the manifestation of their King, one of their own prophets foretold that when He did appear men would hide their faces from Him and esteem Him not? Finally, what explanation have we to offer for the fact that such things *were* predicted centuries before He came to this earth and that they *were* literally fulfilled to the very letter? As another has said, "No prediction could have seemed more improbable, and yet none ever received a sadder and more complete fulfillment."

We pass on now to those predictions which have reference to the *death of our Lord*. If it was wonderful that an Israelitish prophet should foretell the rejection of the Messiah by His own nation, what shall we say to the fact that the Old Testament Scriptures prophesied in detail concerning *the manner or form of His death*? Yet again and again we find this to be the case! Let us examine a few typical instances.

First, it was intimated that our Lord should be betrayed and sold for the price of a common slave. In Zechariah 11:12 we read, "*So they weighed for My price thirty pieces of silver.*" Who was it that was able to declare, centuries before the event came to pass, the exact amount that Judas should receive for his dastardly deed? In Isaiah 53:7 we have another line in this marvelous picture which human wisdom could not possibly have supplied—"*He is brought as a lamb to the slaughter, and as a sheep before her shearers is dumb, so He opened not His mouth.*" Who could have foreseen this most unusual sight of a prisoner standing before his judges with his life at stake, yet attempting and offering no defense? Yet this is precisely what did happen in connection with our Lord, for we are told in Mark 15:5, "*But Jesus yet answered nothing; so that Pilate marveled.*" Again; who was it that knew seven hundred years before the greatest tragedy of human history was enacted that the Son of God, the King of the Jews, the gentlest and meekest Man who ever trod our earth, should be scourged and spat upon? Yet such an experience *was* foretold: "*I gave My back to the smiters, and My cheeks to them that plucked off the hair: I hid not My face from shame and spitting"* (Isaiah 50:6).

Further; the form of capital punishment reserved for Jewish criminals was stoning to death, and in David's time the experience of crucifixion was entirely unknown, yet we find in Psalm 22:16 that Israel's king was inspired to write, *"They pierced My hands and My feet!"* Again; what human foresight could have seen that in His thirst-agonies upon the cross our Lord should be given gall and vinegar to drink? Yet it was declared a thousand years before the Lord of Glory was nailed to the tree that, *"They gave Me also gall for My meat; and in My thirst they gave Me vinegar to drink."* (Psalm 69:21). Finally; we ask, how could David foretell, unless he was inspired by the Holy Spirit, that our Lord should be taunted by His enemies and challenged to come down from the Cross? Yet in Psalm 22:7–8 we read, *"All they that see Me laugh Me to scorn: they shoot out the lip, they shake the head, saying, He trusted on the Lord that He would deliver Him: let Him deliver Him, seeing He delighted in Him."* Such examples as the above might be multiplied indefinitely, but sufficient illustrations have already been given to warrant us in saying that the fulfilled prophecies of the Bible bespeak the omniscience of its Author.

Were it necessary, and had we the space at our command, scores of additional fulfilled prophecies relating to the History of Israel, the Course of the Gentiles, and the Experiences of the Church—prophecies just as definite, accurate, and remarkable as those relating to the Person of the Lord Jesus Christ—could be given, but our present limits and purpose forbid us so doing.

Having examined a few of the startling prophecies which

treat of the Birth and Death of our Savior, it now only remains for us to apply in a word the significance of this argument. Many have read over these Scriptures before and perhaps have regarded them as being wonderfully descriptive of the Advent and Passion of Jesus Christ, but how many have carefully weighed the fact that each of these Scriptures were in indisputable existence more than five hundred years before our Lord came to this earth?

Man is unable to predict accurately events which are but twenty-four hours distant; only the Divine Mind could have foretold the future, centuries before it came to be. Hence, we affirm with the utmost confidence that the hundreds of fulfilled prophecies in the Bible attest and demonstrate the truth that the Scriptures are the inspired, infallible, inerrant Word of God.

6. The Typical Significance of the Scriptures Declare Their Divine Authorship

"*In the volume of the Book it is written of Me*" (Hebrews 10:7). Christ is the Key to the Scriptures. Said He, "*Search the Scriptures...they are they which testify of Me*" (John 5:39), and the "*Scriptures*" to which He had reference, were not the four Gospels for they were not then written, but the writings of Moses and the prophets. The Old Testament Scriptures then are something more than a compilation of historical records, something more than a system of social and religious legislation, something more than a code of ethics. The Old Testament Scriptures are fundamentally a stage on which is shown forth in vivid symbolism and ritualism the whole plan of redemption. The events recorded in the Old Testament were actual occurrences, yet they were also typical prefigurations. Throughout the Old Testament dispensations God caused to be shadowed forth in parabolic representation the whole work of redemption by means of a constant and vivid appeal to the senses. This was in full accord with a fundamental law in the economy of God. Nothing is brought to maturity at once. As it is in the natural world, so it is in the spiritual: there is first the blade, then the ear, and then the full corn in the ear. Concerning the Person and work of the Lord Jesus, God first gave a series of pictorial representations, later a large number of specific prophecies, and last of all, when the fullness of time was come, God sent forth His own Son.

It is failure to discern the typical import of the Old Testament Scriptures which has caused so great a part of them to be slighted by so many readers of the Bible. To multitudes of people the Pentateuch is little more than a compilation of effete and meaningless ceremonial rites, and if there is nothing in them more excellent than their outward semblance, then, surely, it is passing strange that they should find a place in *the Word of God*. Take Christ out of Old Testament ritual and you are left with nothing but the dry and empty shell of a nut. It is therefore a matter of small surprise that those who see so little of Christ in the Old Testament Scriptures should undervalue the instruction and edification to be derived from every part of them, and that they entertain such degrading ideas of their inspiration. Deny that there is a *spiritual* meaning in all the laws and customs of the Israelites and what food for the soul can be gathered from a study of them? Deny that they are so many typical representations of Christ and His Sacrifice for sin and you cast reproach on the name and wisdom of God by suggesting that He instituted the carnal ordinances, the cumbrous ceremonies, the propitiations by sacrifice of animals, which are recorded in the opening Books of the Bible.

The typical import and the spiritual value of the Jewish economy, both as a whole and in its many parts, *is expressly affirmed in the New Testament.* The Apostle Paul, when referring to the narratives and events recorded in the Old Testament, declares that, *"Whatsoever things were written aforetime were written for our learning"* (Romans 15:4). Later, when making mention of Israel's exodus from Egypt and their journey through the wilderness, he affirms, *"Now these things were our examples"* and *"Now all these things happened unto them for ensamples:* [marg. *"types"*] *and they are written for our admonition"* (1 Corinthians 10:6-11). Again; when commenting upon, and while expounding the spiritual significance of the Tabernacle, he declares that it was *"the example and shadow of heavenly things"* (Hebrews 8:5). In the next chapter he declares, *"The Tabernacle...was a figure for the time then present"* (Hebrews 9:8-9) and in Hebrews 10, he states, *"The law"* had *"a shadow of good things to come"* (v. 1). From these declarations it is evident that God Himself caused the Tabernacle to be erected exactly according to the pattern which He had showed Moses, for the express purpose that it should be a type for symbolizing heavenly things. Hence it becomes our privilege and bounden duty to seek by the help of the Holy Spirit to ascertain the meaning of the types of the Old Testament.

In addition to the express declarations of the New Testament quoted above, there are a number of additional passages which also teach the same thing. John the Baptist hailed our Savior as *"The Lamb of God which taketh away the sin of the world"* (John 1:29), that is, *as the great Antitype* of the sacrificial lambs of Old Testament ritual. In His discourse with Nicodemus our Lord alluded to the lifting up of the Brazen Serpent in the wilderness as a type of His own lifting up on the Cross (John 3:14). Writing to the Corinthians the Apostle Paul said, *"Christ our Passover is sacrificed for us"* (1 Corinthians 5:7), thus signifying that Exodus 12 pointed forward to the Lord Jesus. Writing to the Galatians the same Apostle makes mention of the history of Abraham, his wives and his children, and then states *"which things are an allegory"* (Galatians 4:24). Now there are many brethren who will own the typical significance of *these* things, but who refuse to acknowledge that anything else in the Old Testament has a typical meaning save those which are expressly interpreted in the New. But this we conceive to be a mistake and to place a limit upon the scope and value of the Word of God. Rather let us regard those Old Testament types which *are* expounded in the New Testament as *samples of* others which are not explained. Are there no more prophecies in the Old Testament than those which, in the New Testament, are said to be "fulfilled"? Assuredly. Then let us admit the same concerning the types.

Several volumes would be filled were we to dwell upon everything in the Old Testament which has a typical meaning and spiritual application. All we can now attempt is to single out a few illustrations as samples, leaving our readers to pursue further this entrancing study for themselves.

The very first chapter of Genesis is rich in its spiritual contents. Not only does it give us the only reliable and authentic account of the creation of this world, but it also reveals God's order in the work of the new creation. In Genesis 1:1 we have the *original* or primitive creation—*"in the beginning"*. Not only do we have the history of the earth, but also the history of man. In the beginning he was created by God—created in the image and likeness of his Maker. But a terrible calamity followed. An enemy appeared on the scene. The heart of the creature was seduced, unbelief and disobedience being the consequence. Man fell, and awful was his fall. God's image was broken: human nature was ruined by sin: desolation and death took the place of God's likeness and life. In consequence of his sin, man's mind was blinded and darkness rested upon the face of his understanding.

Also, we read in Genesis 1, the work of God bringing light into the world. "*The Spirit of God moved upon the face of the waters. And God said, Let there be light: and there was light*" (vv. 3-4). The parallel holds good in regeneration. In the work of the new birth which is performed within the darkened and spiritually dead sinner, the Spirit of God is the prime mover, convicting the soul of its lost and ruined condition and revealing the need of the appointed Savior. The instrument that He employs is the written Word, the Word of God, and in every genuine conversion God says, "Let there be light," and there is light. "*For God, who commanded the light to shine out of darkness, hath shined in our hearts, to give the light of the knowledge of the glory of God in the face of Jesus Christ*" (2 Corinthians 4:6). The parallel might be followed much further, but sufficient has been said to show that beneath the actual history of Genesis 1 may be discerned by the anointed eye the spiritual history of the believer's new creation, and as such it bears the stamp of its Divine Author and evidences the fact that the opening chapter of the Bible is no mere human compilation.

In the coats of skin with which the Lord God clothed our first parents, we have an incident that is full of spiritual instruction and which could never have been invented by man. To obtain these skins life had to be taken, blood had to be shed, the innocent (animals) must die in the place of Adam and Eve who were guilty, so as to provide a covering for them. Thus, the Gospel truths of redemption by bloodshedding and salvation through a substitutionary sacrifice were preached in Eden. Be it noted that man did not have to provide a covering for himself any more than the "prodigal son" did, nor were they asked to clothe themselves any more than was he: in the one case we read, "*The Lord God made coats of skins and clothed them*" (Genesis 3:21), and in the other the command was, "*Bring forth the best robe, and put it on him*" (Luke 15:22), and both speak of "*the robe of righteousness*" (Isaiah 61:10) which is furnished in Christ.

In the offerings which Cain and Abel presented to the Lord, and in the response which they met with, we discover a foreshadowing of New testament truths. Abel brought of the firstlings of the flock with their fat. He recognized that he was alienated from God and could not draw nigh to Him without a suitable offering. He saw that his own life was forfeited through sin, that justice clamored for his death, and that his only hope lay in another (*a lamb*) dying in his stead. By faith Abel presented his bloody offering to God and it was accepted. On the other hand, Cain refused to take the place of a lost sinner before God. He refused to acknowledge that death was his due. He refused to place his confidence in a sacrificial substitute. He brought as an offering to God the fruits of the ground—the product of his own labors and in consequence, his offering was rejected. Thus, at the commencement of human history we have shown forth the fact that salvation is by grace through faith and altogether apart from works (Ephesians 2:8-9).

In the great Deluge and the ark in which Noah and his house found shelter, we have a typification of great spiritual verities. From them we learn that God takes cognizance of the doings of His creatures; that He is holy and sin is abhorrent to Him; that His righteousness requires Him to punish sin and destroy sinners. Yet, here also we learn that in judgment God remembers mercy, that He has no pleasure in the death of the wicked; that His grace provides a refuge if only His sinful creatures will avail themselves of His provision. Yet only in one place can deliverance from the Divine wrath be found. In the ark alone is safety and security. And, in like manner, today, there is only one Savior for sinners, and that is the Lord Jesus Christ, *"Neither is there salvation in any other: for there is none other name under heaven given among men, whereby we must be saved"* (Acts 4:12).

In the deliverance of Israel from Egypt and their wilderness journey, we see portrayed the history of God's people in the present dispensation. We, too, were living in a world without God and without hope (Ephesians 2:12). We, too, were in bondage to the cruel taskmasters of sin and Satan. We, too, were in imminent danger of falling beneath the sword of the avenging Angel of Justice. But, for us, too, a way of escape was provided. For us, too, a Lamb was slain. Unto us, too, was given the precious promise, *"When I see the blood I will pass over you"* (Exodus 12:13). And we, too, were redeemed by Almighty power and were *"delivered from the power of darkness and translated into the kingdom of God's dear Son"* (Colossians 1:13)

After our exodus from Egypt there lies before us a pilgrim journey through a barren and hostile wilderness as we journey toward the Promised Land. We have to pass through a strange country and meet with enemy forces, that we are unable to overcome in our own strength. For these tasks, our own resources—the things we brought with us out of Egypt—are altogether inadequate, and thus we, too, are cast upon the sufficiency of Israel's God. And blessed be His name, ample provision is made for us and grace is furnished for every need. For us there is heavenly manna in the exceeding great and precious promises of God. For us there comes water out of the Smitten Rock in the person of the Holy Spirit (John 7:38-39) who refreshes our souls by taking of the things of Christ and showing them unto us and who strengthens us with might in the inner man. For us too, there is a pillar of cloud and fire to guide us by day and by night in the Holy Scriptures, which are a lamp unto our feet and a light unto our path. For us, too, there is One to counsel and direct us, to intercede for us and help us overcome our Amalekites in the Captain of our salvation who has said, "Lo, I am with you alway, even unto the end." And, at the close of our pilgrimage we shall enter a fairer land than that which flowed with milk and honey for we have been begotten "to an inheritance incorruptible and undefiled, and that faded not away, reserved in heaven" for us.

Let the careful and impartial reader weigh thoroughly what has been said above, and surely it is evident that the numerous resemblances between the story of Israel and the spiritual history of God's children in this dispensation cannot be so many coincidences, and can only be accounted for on the ground that the writings of Moses were inspired by the Living God.

The history of Israel in Canaan as the professed people of God corresponds with the history of the professing church in the New Testament dispensation. After Moses, the one who led Israel out from their Egyptian bondage, came Joshua, who led Israel in their conquest of Canaan. So after our Lord left this earth, He sent the Holy Spirit who through the Apostles caused the Jericho's and Ai's of Paganism to be overthrown and the greater part of the world to be evangelized. But after their occupancy of Canaan Israel's history was a sad one, being characterized by spiritual declination and departure from God. So it was with the professing church. Very quickly after the death of the Apostles heresy corrupted the Christian profession, and just as Israel of old grew tired of a theocracy and demanded a human head and king, like the nations which surrounded them, so the professing church became dissatisfied with the New Testament form of church government and submitted to the domination of a pope. And just as Israel's kings became more and more corrupt until God would bear with them no longer and sold His people into captivity, so after the setting up of the Papal See there followed the long period of the Dark Ages when Europe was subjected to a spiritual bondage and when the Word of God was bound in chains. Then, just as God raised up Ezra and Nehemiah to recover the living oracle and to lead out of their captivity a remnant of His people, so in the sixteenth century, a.d., God raised up Luther and honored contemporaries to bring about the great Reformation of Protestantism. Finally: just as after the days of Ezra and Hehemiah the Jews in Palestine witnessed a marked spiritual declination, ultimately lapsing into the ritualism of the Pharisees and the rationalism of the Sadducees from which God's elect were delivered only by the appearing of His own Son, so has history repeated itself. Since Reformation and the last of the Puritans, Christendom has moved swiftly in the direction of the predicted apostasy, and today we have reproduced the ancient Pharisee-ism in the rapid spread of Roman Catholicism, and the ancient Sadducee-ism in the far-reaching effects of the infidelity of Higher Criticism: and as it was before, so it will be again—God's elect will be delivered only by the reappearing of our Lord and Savior Jesus Christ.

Thus we see how wonderfully and accurately the Old testament history runs parallel with and anticipated the history of the professing church in the New Testament dispensation. It has been truly said that "Coming events cast their shadows before them," and who but He who knows the end from the beginning and who upholds all things by the word of His power, could have caused the shadow of the Old Testament to have taken the shape they did, and thus give a true and comprehensive parabolic setting forth of that which has taken place thousands of years later!

But not only do the broad outlines of Old Testament history possess a typical meaning, everything in the Old Testament Scriptures has a spiritual value.

Every battle fought by the Israelites, every change in the administration of their government, every detail in their elaborate ceremonialism, and every personal biography narrated in the Bible, is designed for our instruction and edification. The Bible contains nothing that is superfluous. From beginning to end the Scriptures testify of Christ.

Inanimate objects like the ark, which tells of security in Christ from the storms of Divine wrath; like the manna, which speaks of Him as the Bread of Life; like the brazen Serpent uplifted on the pole, of the Tabernacle, which presents Him as the meeting place of God and men—all foreshadowed the Redeemer. Living creatures like the Passover Lamb, the sacrificial bullocks, goats and rams, all pointed forward in general and in detail to the great Sacrifice for sins. Institutions like the Passover, which prefigured His death; like the waving of the first-fruits, which forecast His resurrection; like the fast of Pentecost with its two loaves baked with leaven, telling of the uniting into one Body of the Jew and the Gentile; like the Burnt, the Meal and the Peace "sweet savor" offerings, which proclaimed the excellency of Christ's person in the esteem of God—all emblemized our blessed Savior. And, many of the leading personages of Old Testament biography gave a remarkable delineation of our Lord's character and earthly ministry.

Abel was a type of Christ. His name signifies vanity and emptiness which foreshadowed the Lord Jesus who *"made Himself of no reputation,"* literally *"emptied Himself"* (Philippians 2:7), when He assumed the nature of man who is *"like unto vanity"* (Psalms 72:9). By calling, Abel, was a shepherd, and it was in his shepherd character he brought an offering to God, namely, the firstlings of his flock—speaking of the Good Shepherd who offered Himself to God. The offering which Abel brought to God is termed an *"excellent"* one (Hebrews 11:4) and as such it pointed forward to the *precious blood* of Christ, the value of which cannot be estimated in silver and gold. Abel's offering was accepted by God, God "*testifying*" His approval of it; and, in like manner, God publicly witnessed to His acceptance of Christ's sacrifice when He raised Him from the Dead (Acts 2:32). Abel's offering still *speaks* to God—"*by it he being dead, yet speaketh;*" so, too, Christ's offering "speaks" to God (Hebrews 12:24). Though guilty of no offense, Abel was hated by his brother and cruelly slain at his hand, foreshadowing the treatment which the Lord Jesus received at the hands of the Jews—His brethren according to the flesh.

Isaac was a type of Christ. he was the child of promise. His nativity was announced by an angel. He was supernaturally begotten. He was born at an appointed time. He was named by God (Genesis 1:18-19). He was the "*seed*" to whom the promises were made and through whom they were secured. He became obedient unto death. He carried on his own shoulder the wood on which he was to be offered. He was securely fastened to the alter. He was presented as a sacrifice to God. He was offered on Mount Moriah—the same on which, two thousand years later, Jesus Christ was offered. And, it was on the "*third day*" that Abraham received him back "*in a figure*" from the dead (Hebrews 11:19).

Joseph is a type of Christ. He was Jacob's well-beloved son. He readily responded to his father's will when asked to go on a mission to his brethren. While seeking his brethren he became a "*wanderer in the field*" (Genesis 37:15)—the "*field*" figuring the world (see Matthew 13:38). He found his brethren in Dothan, which signifies the law—so the Lord Jesus found His brethren under the bondage of the law. His brethren mocked and refused to receive him. His brethren took counsel together against him that they might put him to death. Judah (Judas is the Greek form of the same word) advised his brethren to sell Joseph to the Ishmaelites. After he had been rejected by his brethren, Joseph was taken down into Egypt in order that he might become a Saviour to the world. While in Egypt, Joseph was tempted, not without any compromise he put from him the evil solicitation. He was falsely accused and through no fault of his own was cast into prison. There he was the interpreter of dreams—the one who threw light on what was mysterious. In prison he became the savor of life to the butler, and the savor of death to the baker. After a period of humiliation and shame, he was exalted to the throne of Egypt. From that throne he administered bread to a hungering and perishing humanity. Subsequently, Joseph became known to his brethren, and in fulfillment of what he had previously announced to them, they bowed down before him and owned his sovereignty.

Moses was a type of Christ. Moses became the adopted son of Pharaoh's daughter—so that legally he had a mother but *no father*, thus typifying our Lord's miraculous birth of a virgin. During infancy, his life was endangered by the evil designs of the ruler. Like Christ, his early life was spent in Egypt. Later, he renounced the position of royalty, refusing to be called the son of Pharaoh's daughter; and he who was rich, for the sake of his people, became poor. Before he commenced His life's work, a long period was spent in Midian in obscurity. Here he received a call and commission from God to go to deliver his brethren out of their terrible bondage. The credentials of his mission were seen in the miracles which he performed. Though despised and rejected by the rulers in Egypt, he, nevertheless, succeeded in delivering his own people. Subsequently, he became the leader and head of all Israel. In character he was the meekest man in all the earth. In all God's house, he was faithful as a servant. In the wilderness, he sent twelve men to spy out Canaan as our Lord sent out the twelve Apostles to preach the Gospel. He fasted for forty days. On the mount he was transfigured so that the skin of his face shone. He acted as God's prophet to the people, as the people's intercessor before God. He was the only man mentioned in the Old Testament that was prophet, priest and king. He was the giver of a Law, the builder of a Tabernacle, and the organizer of a Priesthood. His last act was to "bless the people" (Deuteronomy 33:29), as our Lord's last act was to *"bless"* His disciples (Luke 24:50).

Samson was a type of Christ—see the Book on Judges. An angel announced his birth (13:3). From birth he was a Nazarite (13:5)—separated to God. Before he was born it was promised that he should be a savior to Israel (13:5). He was treated unkindly by his own nation (15:11-13). He was delivered up to the Gentiles by his own countrymen (15:12). He was mocked and cruelly treated by the Gentiles (16:19-21, 25) yet he was a mighty deliverer of Israel. His miracles were performed under the power of the Holy Spirit (14:19). He accomplished more in his death than he did in his life (16:30). He was imprisoned in the enemy's stronghold; the gates were barred, and a watch was set; yet, rising up at midnight, in the early hours of the morning—*"a great while before day"*—he burst the bars, broke open the gate, and issued forth triumphant—a remarkable type of our Lord's resurrection. He occupied the position of *"judge,"* as our Lord will in the last great day.

David was a type of Christ. He was born in Bethlehem.

He is described as *"of a beautiful countenance and goodly to look upon"* (2 Samuel 16:12). His name means "the beloved." By occupation, he was a shepherd. During his life of shepherding, he entered into conflict with wild beasts. He slew Goliath—the opposer of God's people and a type of Satan. From the obscurity of shepherd-hood he was exalted to Israel's throne. He was anointed as king *before* he was coronated. He was preeminently a man of prayer (see the Psalms) and is the only one in Scripture termed "a *man after*" God's "*own heart*" (Acts 13:22). He was a man of sorrows and acquainted with grief, suffering chiefly from those of his own household. Repeated attempts were made upon his life by Israel's ruler. When his enemy (Saul) was in his power he refused to slay him, instead, he dealt with him in mercy and grace. He delivered Israel from all their enemies and vanquished all their foes.

Solomon was a type of Christ. He was Israel's king. His name signifies "*Peaceable*," and he foreshadows *the millennial reign of the Lord Jesus* when He shall rule as Prince of Peace. He was chosen and ordained of God before he was crowned. He rode upon another's mule, not as a warrior, but as the king of peace in lowly guise (1 Kings 1:33). Gentiles took part in the coronation of Solomon (1 Kings 1:38) typifying the *universal* homage which Christ shall receive during the millennium. The Cherethites and Pelethites were soldiers, so that Solomon was followed by an army at the time of his coronation (1 Kings 1:33; Rev. 19:11). Solomon began his reign by showing mercy to and yet demanding righteousness from Adonijah (1 Kings 1:51)—such will be the leading characteristics of Christ's millennial government. Solomon was the builder of Israel's Temple

(Acts 15:16). At the dedication of the Temple, Solomon was the one who offered sacrifices unto the Lord: thus the king fulfilled the office of priest (1 Kings 8:63), which typifies the Lord Jesus who "shall be a Priest upon His throne" (Zech. 6:13). Solomon's *"fame"* went abroad far and wide and *"all the earth sought to Solomon"* (1 Kings 10:24). The queen of Sheba, representing the *Gentiles*, came up to Jerusalem to pay him homage (1 Kings 10) as all the nations will to Christ during the millennium (see Zech. 14:16). All Israel's land enjoyed rest and peace. The glory and magnificence of Solomon's reign has never been equaled before or since—"*And the Lord magnified Solomon exceedingly in the sight of all Israel, and bestowed upon him such royal majesty as had not been on any king before him in Israel*" (1 Chronicles 29:25).

In the above types we have not sought to be exhaustive but suggestive by singling out only the leading lines in each typical picture. There are many other Old Testament characters who were types of Christ which we cannot now consider at length:—Adam typified His Headship; Enoch His Ascension; Noah as the provider of a Refuge; Jacob as the one who served for a Wife; Aaron as the great High Priest; Joshua as the Captain of our salvation; Samuel as the Faithful Prophet; Elijah as the Miracle worker; Jeremiah as the despised and rejected Servant of God; Daniel as the Faithful Witness for God; Jonah as the One raised from the dead on the third day.

In closing this chapter, let us apply the argument. Of the many typical persons in the Old Testament who prefigure the Lord Jesus Christ, the striking, the accurate, and the manifold lights, in which each exhibits Him is truly remarkable. No two of them represent Him from exactly the same viewpoint. Each one contributes a line or two to the picture, but all are needed to give a complete delineation. That an authentic *history* should supply a series of personages in different ages, whose characters, offices, and histories, should exactly correspond with those of Another who did not appear upon earth until centuries later, can only be accounted for on the supposition of Divine appointment. When we consider the utter dissimilarity of these typical persons to one another; when we note that they had little or nothing in common with each other; when we remember that each of them represents some peculiar feature in a composite Anti type; we discover that we have a literary phenomenon which is truly remarkable. Abel, Isaac, Joseph, Moses, Samson, David, Solomon (and all the others) are each deficient when viewed separately; but when looked at in conjunction they form an harmonious whole, and give us a complete representation of our Lord's miraculous birth, His peerless character, His life's mission, His sacrificial death, His triumphant resurrection, His ascension to heaven, and His millennial reign. Who could have invented such character? How remarkable that the earliest history in the world, extending from the creation and reaching to the last of the prophets—written by various hands through a period of fifteen centuries—should from start to finish concentrate in a single point, and that point the person and work of the blessed Redeemer! Verily, *such a Book must have been written by God*—no other conclusion is possible. Beneath the historical we discern the spiritual: behind the incidental we behold the typical: underneath the human biographies we see the form of Christ, and in these things we discover on every page of the Old Testament the "watermark" of heaven.

7. The Wonderful Unity of the Bible Attests its Divine Authorship

The manner in which the Bible has been produced argues against its unity. The Bible was penned on two continents, written in three languages, and its composition and compilation extended through the slow progress of sixteen centuries. The various parts of the Bible were written at different times and under the most varying circumstances. Parts of it were written in tents, deserts, cities, palaces and dungeons; in times of imminent danger and in seasons of ecstatic joy. Among its writers were judges, kings, priests, prophets, patriarchs, prime ministers, herdsmen, scribes, soldiers, physicians and fishermen. Yet despite these varying circumstances, conditions and workmen, the Bible is *one* Book, behind its many parts there is an unmistakable organic unity. It contains *one* system of doctrine, *one* code of ethics, *one* plan of salvation and *one* rule of faith.

Now if forty different men were selected today from such varying stations and callings of life as to include clerks, rulers, politicians, judges, clergy, doctors, farm laborers and fishermen, and each was asked to contribute a chapter for some book on theology or church government, when their several contributions were collected and bound together, would there be any unity about them, could that book truly be said to be *one book*; or would not their different productions vary so much in literary value, diction and matter as to be merely a heterogeneous mass, a miscellaneous collection? Yet we do not find this to be the case in connection with God's Book. Although the Bible is a volume of sixty-six Books, written by forty different men, treating of such a large variety of themes as to cover nearly the whole range of human inquiry, we find it is *one* Book, the Book (not the *books*), the Bible.

Further; if we were to select specimens of literature from the third, fifth, tenth, fifteenth and twentieth centuries of the Christian era and were to bind them together, what unity and harmony should we find in such a collection? Human writers reflect the spirit of their own day and generation and the compositions of men living amid widely differing influences and separated by centuries of time have little or nothing in common with each other. Yet although the earliest portions of the Sacred Canon date back to at least the fifteenth century, b.c., while the writings of John were not completed till the close of the first century, AD, nevertheless, we find a perfect harmony throughout the Scriptures from the first verse in Genesis to the last verse in Revelation. The great ethical and spiritual lessons presented in the Bible, by whoever taught, *agree*.

The more one really studies the Bible the more one is convinced that behind the many human mouths there is One overruling, controlling Mind. Imagine forty persons of different nationalities, possessing various degrees of musical culture visiting the organ of some cathedral and at long intervals of time, and without any collusion whatever, striking sixty-six different notes, which when combined yielded the theme of the grandest oratorio ever heard: would it not show that behind these forty different men there was one presiding mind, one great Tone master? As we listen to some great orchestra, with an immense variety of instruments playing their different parts, but producing melody and harmony, we realize that at the back of these many musicians there is the personality and genius of the composer. And when we enter the halls of the Divine Academy and listen to the heavenly choirs singing the Song of Redemption, all in perfect accord and unison, we know that it is God Himself who has written the music and put this song into their mouths.

We now submit two illustrations which demonstrate the unity of the Holy Scriptures. Certain grand conceptions run through the entire Bible like a cord on which are strung so many precious pearls. First and foremost among them is the Divine Plan of Redemption. Just as the scarlet thread runs through all the cordage of the British Navy, so a crimson aura surrounds every page of God's Word.

In the Scriptures the Plan of Redemption is central and fundamental. In Genesis, we have recorded the Creation and Fall of man to show that he has the capacity for and is in need of redemption. Next we find the Promise of the Redeemer, for man requires to have before him the hope and expectation of a Savior. Then follows an elaborate system of sacrifices and offerings and these represent pictorially the nature of redemption and the condition under which salvation is realized. At the commencement of the New Testament we have the four Gospels and they set forth the Basis of Redemption, namely, the Incarnation,

Life, Death, Resurrection and Ascension of the Redeemer. Next comes the Book of the Acts which illustrates again and again the Power of Redemption, showing that it is adequate to work its great results in the salvation of both Jew and Gentile. Finally, in the Revelation, we are shown the ultimate triumphs of redemption, the Goal of Salvation—the redeemed dwelling with God in perfect union and communion. Thus, we see that though a large number of human media were employed in the writing of the Bible, yet their productions are not independent of each other, but are complementary and supplementary parts of one great whole; that one sublime truth is common to them all, namely, man's need of redemption and God's provision of a Redeemer. And the only explanation of this fact is, that "*All Scripture is given by inspiration of God*" (2 Timothy 3:16).

Secondly; among all the many personalities presented in the Bible, we find that one stands out above all others, not merely prominent but preeminent. Just as in the scene unveiled in the fifth chapter of the Revelation, we find the Lamb in the center of the heavenly throngs, so we find that in the Scriptures also, the Lord Jesus Christ is accorded the place which alone befits His unique Person. Considered from one standpoint the Scriptures are really the biography of the Son of God.

In the Old Testament we have the *Promise* of our Lord's Incarnation and Mediatorial work. In the Gospels we have the *Proclamation* of His Mission and the *Proofs* of His Messianic claims and authority. In the Acts we have a demonstration of His saving *Power* and the execution of His missionary *Program*. In the Epistles we find an exposition and amplification of His *Precepts* for the education of His

People. While in the Apocalypse, we behold the unveiling or *Presentation* of His *Person* and the *Preparation* of the earth for His *Presence*. The Bible is therefore seen to be peculiarly the *Book of Jesus Christ*. Christ not only testified to the Scriptures, but each section of the Scriptures testify of Him. Every page of the Holy Book has stamped upon it His photograph and every chapter bears His autograph. He is its one great theme, and the only explanation of this fact is that, the Holy Spirit superintended the work of each and every writer of the Scriptures.

The unity of the Scriptures is further to be seen on the fact that they are entirely free from any real contradictions. Though different writers often described the same incidents—as, for example, the four evangelists recording the facts relating to our Lord's ministry and redemptive work—and though there is considerable variety in the narrations of these, yet there are no real discrepancies. The harmony existing between them does not appear on the surface, but, often, is only discovered by protracted study, though it is there nevertheless. Moreover, there is a perfect agreement of doctrine between all the writers in the Bible. The teaching of the prophets and the teaching of the Apostles on the great truths of God's righteousness, the demands of His holiness, the utter ruin of man, the exceeding sinfulness of sin, and the way of salvation, is entirely harmonious. This might appear a thing easily effected. But those who are acquainted with human nature, and have read widely the writings of men, will acknowledge that nothing but the inspiration of the writers can explain this fact. Nowhere can we find two uninspired writers, however similar they may have been in their religious sentiments, who agree in all points of doctrine. Nay, the entire consistency of sentiment is not to be found even in the writings of the same author at different periods. In his later years Spurgeon's statement of some doctrines was much more modified than the utterances of his earlier days. Increasing knowledge causes men to change their views upon many subjects. But among the writers of Scripture there is the most perfect harmony, because they obtained their knowledge of truth and duty not by the efforts of study, but from inspiration by the Holy Spirit of God.

When therefore we find that in the productions of forty different men there is perfect accord and concord, unison and unity, harmony in all their teachings, and the same conceptions pervading all their writings, the conclusion is irresistible that behind their minds, and guiding their hands, there was the master-mind of God Himself. Does not the unity of the Bible illustrate the Divine Inspiration of the Bible and demonstrate the truth of its own assertion that *"God, who at sundry times and in divers manners spake in time past unto the fathers by the prophets"* (Hebrews 1:1)?

8. The Marvelous Influence of the Bible Declares its Super-Human Character

The influence of the Bible is world wide. Its mighty power has affected every department of human activity. The contents of the Scriptures have supplied themes for the greatest poets, artists and musicians which the world has yet produced, and have been the mightiest factor of all in shaping the moral progress of the race. Let us consider a few examples of the Bible's influence as displayed in the various realms of human enterprise.

Take away such sublime oratorios as "Elijah" and "The Messiah," and you have taken out of the realm of music something which can never be duplicated; destroy the countless hymns which have drawn their inspiration from the Scriptures and you have left us little else worth singing. Eliminate from the compositions of Tennyson, Wordsworth and Carlisle every reference to the moral and spiritual truths taught in God's Word and you have stripped them of their beauty and robbed them of their fragrance. Take down from off the walls of our best Art Galleries those pictures which portray scenes and incidents in the history of Israel and the life of our Lord and you have removed the richest gems from the crown of human genius. Remove from our statute books every law which is founded upon the ethical conceptions of the Bible and you have annihilated the greatest factor in modern civilization. Rob our libraries of every book which is devoted to the work of elaborating and disseminating the precepts and concepts of Holy Writ and you have taken from us that which cannot be valued in dollars and cents.

The Bible has done more for the emancipation and civilization of the heathen than all the forces which the human arm can wield put together. Someone has said, "Draw a line around the nations which have the Bible and you will then have divided between barbarism and civilization, between thrift and poverty, between selfishness and charity, between oppression and freedom, between life and the shadow of death." Even Darwin had to concede the miraculous element in the triumphs of the missionaries of the cross.

Here are two or three men who land on a savage island. Its inhabitants possess no literature and have no written language. They regard the white man as their enemy and have no desire to be shown *the error of their ways*. They are cannibals by instinct and little better than the brute beasts in their habits of life. The missionaries who have entered their midst have no money with which to buy their friendship, no army to compel their obedience and no merchandise to stir their avarice. Their only weapon is "the Sword of the Spirit," their only capital "the unsearchable riches of Christ," their only offer the invitation of the Gospel. Yet somehow, they succeed, and without the shedding of any blood gain the victory. In a few short years naked savagery is changed to the garb of civilization, lust is transformed into purity, cruelty is now kindness, avarice has become unselfishness, and where before vindictiveness existed there is now to be seen meekness and the spirit of loving self-sacrifice. And this has been accomplished by the Bible! This miracle is still being repeated in every part of the earth! What other book, or library of books, could work such a result? Is it not evident to all that the Book which does exert such a unique and unrivaled influence must be vitalized by the life of God Himself?

This wonderful characteristic, namely the unique influence of the Bible, is rendered the more remarkable when we take into account the antiquity of the Scriptures! The last Books which were added to the Sacred Canon are now more than eighteen hundred years old, yet the workings of the Bible are as mighty in their effects today as they were in the first century of the Christian era.

The power of man's books soon wane and disappear. With but few exceptions, the productions of the human intellect enjoys a brief existence. As a general rule, the writings of man within fifty years of their first public appearance lie untouched on the top shelves of our libraries. Man's writings are like himself—dying creatures. Man comes into the age of this world, plays his part in the drama of life, influences the audience while he is acting, but is forgotten as soon as the curtain falls upon his brief career; so it is with his writings. While they are fresh and new, they amuse, interest or instruct as the wise may be, and then die a natural death. Even the few exceptions to this rule only exert a very limited influence, their power is circumscribed;

they are unread by the great majority, yea, are unknown to the biggest portion of our race. But how different with God's Book! The written Word, like the Living Word, is "The same yesterday, and today, and forever," and unlike any other book it has made its way into all countries and speaks with equal clearness, directness and force to all men in their mother tongue. The Bible never becomes antiquated, its vitality never diminishes and its influence is more irresistible and universal today than it was two thousands years ago. Such facts as these declare with no uncertain voice that the Bible is endued with the same Divine life and energy as its Author, for in no other way can we account for its marvelous influence through the centuries and its mighty power upon the world.

9. The Miraculous Power of the Bible Shows Forth That its Inspirer Is the Almighty

The Power of God's Word to Convict Men of Sin.

In Hebrews 4:12 we have a Scripture which draws attention to this peculiar characteristic of the Bible—"For the Word of God is quick, and powerful, and sharper than any two edged sword, piercing even to the dividing asunder of soul and spirit, and of the joints and marrow, and is a discerner of the thoughts and intents of the heart." The writings of men may sometimes stir the emotions, search the conscience, and influence the human will, but in a manner and degree possessed by no other book, the Bible convicts men of their guilt and lost estate. The Word of God is the Divine mirror, for in it man reads the secrets of his own guilty soul and sees the vileness of his own evil nature. In a way absolutely peculiar to themselves, the Scriptures discern the thoughts and intents of the heart and reveal to men the fact that they are lost sinners and in the presence of a Holy God.

Some thirty years ago there resided in one of the Temples of Thibet, a Buddhist priest who had conversed with no Christian missionary, had heard nothing about the cross of

Christ, and had never seen a copy of the Word of God. One day, while searching for something in the temple, he came across a transcription of Matthew's Gospel, which years before had been left there by a native who had received it from some traveling missionary. His curiosity aroused, the Buddhist priest commenced to read it, but when he reached the eighth verse in the fifth chapter, he paused and pondered over it: "Blessed are the pure in heart: for they shall see God." Although he knew nothing about the righteousness of his Maker, although he was quite ignorant concerning the demands of God's holiness, yet he was there and then convicted of his sins, and a work of Divine grace commenced in his soul. Month after month went by and each day he said to himself, "I shall never see God, for I am impure in heart." Slowly but surely the work of the Holy Spirit deepened within him until he saw himself as a lost sinner; vile, guilty, and undone.

After continuing for more than a year in this miserable condition, the priest one day heard that a "foreign devil" was visiting a town nearby and selling books which spoke about God. The same night, the Buddhist priest fled from the temple and journeyed to the town where the missionary was residing. On reaching his destination he sought out the missionary and at once said to him, "Is it true that only those who are pure in heart will see God?" "Yes," replied the missionary, "but the same Book which tells you that, also tells you *how* you may obtain a pure heart," and then he talked to him about our Lord's atoning work and how that "the blood of Jesus Christ His Son cleanseth us from all sin." Quickly the light of God flooded the soul of the Buddhist priest and he found the peace which "passeth all understanding." Now what other book in the world outside of the Bible contains a sentence or even a chapter which, without the aid of any human commentator, is capable of convincing and convicting a heathen that he is a lost sinner? Does not the fact of the miraculous power of the Bible, which has been illustrated by thousands of fully authenticated cases similar to the above, declare that the Scriptures are the inspired Word of God, vested with the same might as their Omnipotent Author?

The Power of God's Word to Deliver Men From Sin.

A single incident which was brought before the notice of the writer must suffice to illustrate the above mentioned truth.

Some forty years ago, a Christian gentleman stood upon the quay of the Liverpool docks distributing tracts to the sailors. In the course of his work he handed one to a man who was just embarking on a voyage to China, and with an oath the sailor took it, crumpled it up and thrust it into his pocket. Some three weeks after, this sailor was down in his cabin and needing a "spell" with which to light his pipe felt in his pocket for the necessary paper and drew out the little tract which he had received in Liverpool. On recognizing it, he uttered a terrible oath and tore the paper in pieces. One small fragment adhered to his tarry hand and, glancing at it, he saw these words: "Prepare to meet thy God." When relating the incident to the writer, he said, "It was at that moment as though a sword had pierced my heart." "Prepare to meet thy God" rang again and again in his ears, and with a stricken'd conscience he was tormented about his lost condition. Presently he retired for the night, but sleep he could not. In desperation, he got up and dressed and went above and paced the deck. Hour after hour he walked up and down, but try as he might he could not dismiss from his mind the words, "Prepare to meet thy God." For years this man had been a helpless slave in the grip of strong drink and knowing his weakness he said: "How can I prepare to meet God, when I am so powerless to overcome my besetting sin?" Finally, he got down upon his knees and cried: "O God, have mercy on me, save me from my sins, deliver me from the power of drink and help me prepare for the meeting with Thee." More than thirty-five years after, this converted sailor told the writer that from the night he had read that quotation from God's Word, had prayed that prayer, and had accepted Christ as his Savior from sin, he had never tasted a single drop of intoxicating liquor and had never once had a desire to craving for strong drink. How marvelous is the power of God's Word to deliver men from sin! Truly, as Dr. Torrey has well said, "A Book which will lift men up to God must have come down from God."

The Power of God's Word Over the Human Affections.

In thousands of instances, men and women have been stretched upon the "rack," torn limb from limb, thrown to the wild beasts, and have been burned at the stake rather than abandon the Bible and promise never again to read its sacred pages. For what other book would men and women suffer and die?

More than two hundred years ago when a copy of the Bible was much more expensive than it is in these days, a peasant who lived in the County of Cork, Ireland, heard that a gentleman in his neighborhood had a copy of the New testament in the Irish language. Accordingly he visited this man and asked to be allowed to see it, and after looking at it with great interest begged to be allowed to copy it. Knowing how poor the peasant was the gentleman asked him where he would get his paper and ink from? "I will buy them," was the reply. "And where will you find a place to write?" "If your honor will allow me the use of your hall, I'll come after my day's work is over and copy a little at a time in the evenings." The gentleman was so moved at this man's intense love of the Bible that he gave him the use of his hall and light and provided him with paper and ink as well. True to his purpose and promise, the peasant labored night after night until he had written out a complete copy of the New Testament. Afterwards, a printed copy was given to him, and the written Testament is preserved by the British and Foreign Bible Society. Again, we ask, what other book in the world could obtain such a hold upon the affections and win such love and reverence, and produce such self-sacrificing toil?

10. The Completeness of the Bible Demonstrates its Divine Perfection

The antiquity of the Scriptures argues against their completeness. The compilation of the Bible was completed more than eighteen centuries ago, while the greater part of the world was yet uncivilized. Since John added the capstone to the Temple of God's Truth, there have been many wonderful discoveries and inventions, yet there have been no additions whatever to the moral and spiritual truths contained in the Bible. Today, we know no more about the origin of life, the nature of the soul, the problem of suffering or the future destiny of man than did those who had the Bible eighteen hundred years ago. Through the centuries of the Christian era, man has succeeded in learning many of the secrets of nature and has harnessed her forces to his service, but in the actual revelation of supernatural truth, *nothing new has been discovered*. Human writers cannot supplement the Divine records for they are complete, entire, "wanting nothing."

The Bible needs no addendum. There is more than sufficient in God's Word to meet the temporal and spiritual needs of all mankind. Though written two thousand years ago, the Bible is still "up-to-date," and answers every vital question which concerns the soul of man in our day. The Book of Job was written three thousand years before Columbus discovered America, yet it is as fresh to the heart of man now as though it had only been published ten years ago. The majority of the Psalms were written two thousand five hundred years before President Wilson was born, yet in our day and generation, they are perfectly new and fresh to the human soul. Such facts as these can only be explained on the hypothesis that the Eternal God is the Author of the Bible.

The *adaptation* of the Scriptures is another illustration of their wonderful completeness. To young or old, feeble or vigorous, ignorant or cultured, joyful or sorrowful, perplexed or enlightened, Orientalist or Occidentalist, saint or sinner, the Bible is a source of blessing, will minister to every need, and is able to supply every variety of want. And the Bible is the only Book in the world of which this can be predicted. The writings of Plato may be a source of interest and instruction to the philosophic mind, but they are unsuitable for placing in the hands of a child. Not so with the Bible: the youngest may profit from a perusal of the Sacred Page. The writings of Jerome or Twain may please, for an hour, the man of humor, but they will bring no balm to the sore heart and will speak no words of comfort and consolation to those passing through the waters of bereavement. How different with the Scriptures—never has a heavy heart turned in vain to God's Word for peace! The writings of Shakespeare, Goethe, and Schiller may be of profit to the Western mind, but they convey little of value to the Easterner. Not so with God's Word; it may be translated into any language and will speak with equal clearness, directness, and power to all men in their mother tongue.

To quote Dr. Burrell: "In every heart, down below all other wants and aspirations, there is a profound longing to know the way of spiritual life. The world is crying, "What shall I do to be saved?" Of all books, the Bible is the only one that answers that universal cry. There are other books which set forth morality with more or less correctness; but there is none other that suggests a blotting out of the record of the mis lived past or an escape from the penalty of the broken law. There are other books that have poetry; but there is none that sings the song of salvation or gives a troubled soul the peace that floweth like a river. There are other books that have eloquence; but there is no other that enables us to behold God Himself with outstretched hands pleading with men to turn and live. There are other books that have science; but there is none other that can give the soul a definite assurance of the future life, so that it can say, "I know whom I have believed, and am persuaded that He is able to keep that which I have committed unto Him against that day."

Though other books contain valuable truths, they also have an admixture of error; other books contain part of the truth, the Bible alone contains all the truth. Nowhere in the writings of human genius can a single moral or spiritual truth be found, which is not contained in substance in the Bible. Examine the writings of the ancients; ransack the libraries of Egypt, Assyria, Persia, India, Greece, and Rome; search the contents of the Koran, the Zend—Avesta, or the Bagavad-Gita; gather together the most exalted spiritual thoughts and the sublimest moral conceptions contained in them and you will find that each and all are duplicated in the Bible! Dr. Torrey has said, "If every book but the Bible were destroyed not a single spiritual truth would be lost." In the small compass of God's Word there is stored more wisdom which will endure the test of eternity than the sum total of thinking done by man since his creation. Of all the books in the world, the Bible alone can truly be said to be complete, and this characteristic of the Scriptures is another of the many lines of demonstration which witnesses to the Divine inspiration of the Bible.

11. The Indestructibility of the Bible Is a Proof that its Author Is Divine

The survival of the Bible through the ages is very difficult to explain if it is not in truth the Word of God. Books are like men—dying creatures. A very small percentage of books survive more than twenty years, a yet smaller percentage last a hundred years and only a very insignificant fraction represent those which have lived a thousand years. Amid the wreck and ruin of ancient literature, the Holy Scriptures stand out like the last survivor of an otherwise extinct race, and the very fact of the Bible's continued existence is an indication that like its Author it is indestructible.

When we bear in mind the fact that the Bible has been the special object of never-ending persecution, the *wonder* of the Bible's survival is changed into a *miracle*. Not only has the Bible been the most intensely loved Book in all the world, but it has also been the most bitterly hated. Not only has the Bible received more veneration and adoration than any other book, but it has also been the object of more persecution and opposition. For two thousand years, man's hatred of the Bible has been persistent, determined, relentless and murderous. Every possible effort has been made to undermine faith in the inspiration and authority of the Bible, and innumerable enterprises have been undertaken with the determination to consign it to oblivion. Imperial edicts have been issued to the effect that every known copy of the Bible should be destroyed, and when this measure failed to exterminate and annihilate God's Word then commands were given that every person found with a copy of the Scriptures in his possession should be put to death. The very fact that the Bible has been so singled out for such relentless persecution causes us to wonder at such a unique phenomenon.

Although the Bible is the best Book in the world yet is has produced more enmity and opposition than has the combined contents of all our libraries. Why should this be? Clearly because the Scriptures convict men of their guilt and condemn them for their sins! Political and ecclesiastical powers have united in the attempt to put the Bible out of existence, yet their concentrated efforts have utterly failed. After all the persecution which has assailed the Bible, it is, humanly speaking, a wonder that there is any Bible left at all. Every engine of destruction which human philosophy, science, force, and hatred could bring against a book has been brought against the Bible, yet it stands unshaken and unharmed today. When we remember that no army has defended the Bible and no king has ever ordered its enemies to be extirpated, our wonderment increases. At times nearly all the wise and great of the earth have been pitted together against the Bible, while only a few despised ones have honored and revered it. The cities of the ancients were lighted with bonfires made of Bibles, and for centuries only those in hiding dare read it. How, then, can we account for the survival of the Bible in the face of such bitter persecution? The only solution is to be found in the promise of God. "Heaven and earth shall pass away, but *My Words shall not pass away.*"

The story of the Bible's persecution is an arresting one. During the first three centuries of the Christian era, the Roman Emperor sought to destroy God's Word. One of them, named Diocletian, believed that he had succeeded. He had slain so many Christians and destroyed so many Bibles that when the lovers of the Bible remained quiet for a season and kept in hiding, he imagined that he had made an end of the Scriptures. So elated was he at this achievement, he ordered a medal to be struck inscribed with the words, "The Christian religion is destroyed and the worship of the gods restored." One wonders what that emperor would think if he returned to this earth today and found that more had been written about the Bible than about any other thousand books put together, and that the Bible which enshrines the Christian faith is now translated into more than four hundred languages and is being sent out to every part of the earth!

Centuries after the persecution by the Roman Emperors, when the Roman Catholic Church obtained command of the city of Rome, the Pope and his priests took up the old quarrel against the Bible. The Holy Scriptures were taken away from the people, copies of the Bible were forbidden to be purchased and all who were found with a copy of God's Word in their possession were tortured and killed. For centuries the Roman Catholic Church bitterly persecuted the Bible and it was not until the time of the Reformation at the close of the sixteenth century that the Word of God was again given to the masses in their own tongue.

Even in our day the persecution of the Bible still continues, though the method of attack is changed. Much of our modern scholarship is engaged in the work of seeking to destroy faith in the Divine inspiration and authority of the Bible. In many of our seminaries the rising generation of the clergy are taught that Genesis is a book of myths, that much of the teaching of the Pentateuch is immoral, that the historical records of the Old Testament are unreliable and that the whole Bible is man's creation rather than God's revelation. And so the attack on the Bible is being perpetuated.

Now suppose there was a man who had lived upon this earth for eighteen hundred years, that this man had oftentimes been thrown into the sea and yet could not be drowned; that he had frequently been cast before wild beasts who were unable to devour him; that he had many times been made to drink deadly poisons which never did him any harm; that he had often been bound in iron chains and locked in prison dungeons, yet he had always been able to throw off the chains and escape from his captivity; that he had repeatedly been hanged, till his enemies thought him dead, yet when his body was cut down, he sprang to his feet and walked away as though nothing had happened; that hundreds of times he had been burned at the stake, till there seemed to be nothing left of him, yet as soon as the fires were out he leaped up from the ashes as well and as vigorous as ever—but we need not expand this idea any further; such a man would be super-human, a miracle of miracles. Yet this is exactly how we should regard the Bible! This is practically the way in which the Bible has been treated. It has been burned, drowned, chained, put in prison, and torn to pieces, yet never destroyed!

No other book has provoked such fierce opposition as the Bible, and its preservation is perhaps the most startling miracle connected with it. But two thousand five hundred years ago God declared, *"The grass withereth, the flower fadeth, But the word of our Lord endureth for ever"* (1 Peter 1:24-25). Just as the three Hebrews passed safely through the fiery furnace of Nebuchadnezzar unharmed and unscorched, so the Bible has emerged from the furnace of satanic hatred and assault without even the smell of fire upon it! Just as an earthly parent treasures and lays by the letters received from his child, so our Heavenly Father has protected and preserved the Epistles of love written to His children.

12. Inward Confirmation of the Veracity of the Scriptures

We are living in a day when confidence is lacking; when skepticism and agnosticism are becoming more and more prevalent; and when doubt and uncertainty are made the badges of culture and wisdom. Everywhere men are demanding proof. Hypotheses and speculations fail to satisfy: the heart cannot rest content until it is able to say, "I know." The demand of the human mind is for definite knowledge and positive assurance. And God has condescended to meet this need.

One thing which distinguishes Christianity from all human systems is that it deals with absolute certainties. Christians are people who know. And well it is that they do. The issues concerning life and death are so stupendous; the stake involved in the salvation of the soul is so immense, that we cannot afford to be uncertain here. None but a fool would attempt to cross a frozen river until he was sure that the ice was strong enough to bear him. Dare we then face the river of death with nothing but a vague and uncertain hope to rest upon? Personal assurance is the crying need of the hour. There can be no peace and joy until this is attained. A parent who is in suspense concerning the safety of his child, is in agony of soul. A criminal who lies in the condemned cell hoping for a reprieve is in mental torment until his pardon arrives. And a professed Christian who knows not whether he shall ultimately land in Heaven or Hell, is a pitiable object.

But we say again, real Christians are people who know. They *know* that their Redeemer liveth (John 19:25). They *know* that they have passed from death unto life (1 John 3:14). They *know* that all things work together for good (Romans 8:28). They *know* that if their earthly house of this tabernacle were dissolved; they have a building of God, a house not made with hands, eternal in the heavens (2 Corinthians 5:1). They *know* that one day they shall see Christ face to face and be made like Him (1 John 3:2). In the meantime they *know* whom they have believed, and are persuaded that He is able to keep that which they have committed unto Him against that day (2 Timothy 1:12). If it be asked, *How* do they know, the answer is, they have proven for themselves the trustworthiness of God's Word which affirms these things.

The force of this present argument will appeal to none save those who have an experimental acquaintance with it. In addition to all the external proofs that we have for the Divine Inspiration of the Scriptures, the believer has a source of evidence to which no unbeliever has access. In his own experience, the Christian finds a personal confirmation of the teachings of God's Word. To the man whose life which, judged by the standards of the world, appears morally upright, the statement that "the heart is deceitful above all things and desperately wicked" seems to be the gloomy view of a pessimist, or a description which has no general application. But the believer has found that *"the entrance of Thy words giveth light"* (Psalms 119:130), and in the light of God's Word and beneath the illuminating power of God's Spirit who indwells him, he has discovered there is within him a sink of iniquity. To natural wisdom, which is fond of philosophizing about the freedom of the human will, the declaration of Christ that *"No man can come to Me, except the Father which hath sent Me, draw him"* (John 6:44) seems a hard saying; but, to the one who has been taught by the Holy Spirit something of the binding power of sin, such a declaration has been verified in his own experience. To the one who has done his best to live up to the light which he had, and has sought to develop an honest and amiable character, such a statement as, *"All our righteousnesses are as filthy rags,"* (Isaiah 64:6) seems unduly harsh and severe; but to the man who has received "an unction from the Holy One," his very best works appear to him sordid and sinful; and such they are. The Apostle's confession that *"in me (that is, in my flesh,) dwelleth no good thing"* (Romans 7:18) which once appeared absurd to him, the believer now acknowledges to be his own condition. The description of the Christian which is found in Romans ... is something which none but a regenerate person can understand. The things there mentioned as belonging to the same man at the same time, seem foolish to the wise of this world; but the believer realizes completely the truth of it in his own life.

The promises of God can be tested: their trustworthiness is capable of verification. In the Gospel Christ promises to give rest to all those who are weary and heavy laden that come unto Him. He declares that He came to seek and to save that which was lost. He affirms that *"whosoever drinketh of the water that I shall give him shall never thirst"* (John 4:14). In short, the Gospel presents the Lord Jesus Christ as a Savior. His claim to save can be put to the proof. Yea, it has been, and that by a multitude of individuals that no man can number. Many of these are living on earth today. Every individual who has read in the Scriptures the invitations that are addressed to sinners, and has personally appropriated them to himself, can say n the words of the well-known hymn:—

> "I came to Jesus as I was.
> Weary and worn and sad;
> I found in Him a resting place
> And He has made me glad."

Should these pages be read by a skeptic who, despite his present unbelief, has a sincere and earnest desire to know the truth, he, too may put God's Word to the test and share the experience described above. It is written, *"Believe on the Lord Jesus Christ and thou shalt be saved"* (Acts 16:31)—believe, my reader, and *thou,* too, *shalt* be saved.

"We speak that we do know, and testify that we have seen" (John 3:11). The Bible testifies to the fact that *"all have sinned and come short of the glory of God"* (Romans 3:23), and our own conscience confirms it. The Bible declares that it is *"not by works of righteousness which we have down, but according to His mercy"* (Titus 3:5) God saves us; and the Christian has proven that he was unable to do anything to win God's esteem: but, having cried the prayer of the Publican, he has gone down to his house justified. The Bible teaches that *"if any man be in Christ, he is a new creature:*

old things are passed away; behold, all things are become new;" (2 Corinthians 5:17) and the believer has found that the things he once hated he now loves, and that the things he hitherto counted gain he now regards as dross. The Bible witnesses to the fact that we *"are kept by the power of God through faith,"* (1 Peter 1:5) and the believer has proven that though the world, the flesh, and the devil are arrayed against him, yet the grace of God is sufficient for all his need. Ask the Christian, then, why he believes that the Bible is the Word of God, and he will tell you, Because it has done for me what it professes to do (save); because I have tested its promises for myself; because I find its teachings verified in my own experiences.

To the unregenerate, the Bible is practically a sealed Book. Even the cultured and educated are unable to understand its teachings: parts of it appear plain and simple, but much of it is dark and mysterious. This is exactly what the Bible declares—*"The natural man receiveth not the things of the Spirit of God: for they are foolishness unto him: neither can he know them, because they are spiritually discerned"* (I Corinthians 2:14). But to the man of God, it is otherwise: *"He that believeth on the Son of God hath the witness in himself"* (1 John 5:10). As the Lord Jesus declared, *"If any man will do His will, he shall know of the doctrine"* (John 7:17). While the infidel stumbles in darkness, even in the midst of light, the believer discovers the evidence of its truth in himself with the clearness of a sunbeam. *"For God, who commanded the light to shine out of darkness, hath shined in our hearts, to give the light of the knowledge of the glory of God in the face of Jesus Christ"* (2 Corinthians 4:6).

13. Verbal Inspiration

Not only does the Bible claim to be a Divine revelation, but it also asserts that its original manuscripts were written *"not in the words which man's wisdom teacheth, but which the Holy Spirit teacheth"* (1 Corinthians 2:13). The Bible nowhere claims to have been written by merely *inspired men*—as a matter of fact some of them were very defective characters—Balaam for example—but it insists that the words they uttered and recorded were *God's words*. Inspiration has not primarily to do with the minds of the writers, for many of them understood not what they wrote (1 Peter 1:10–11), but with *the writings* themselves. *"All Scripture is given by inspiration of God"* (2 Timothy 3:16) and *"Scripture"* means *"the writings."* Faith has to do with God's Word and not with the men who wrote it—these are all dead long since, but their writings remain.

A writing that is inspired by God self-evidently implies, in the very expression, that the words are the words of God. To say that the inspiration of the Scriptures applies to their concepts and not to their words; to declare that one part of Scripture is written with one kind or degree of inspiration and another part with another kind or degree, is not only destitute of any foundation or support in the Scriptures themselves, but is repudiated by every statement in the Bible which bears upon the subject now under consideration. To say that the Bible is not the Word of God but merely *contains* the Word of God is the figment of an ill-employed ingenuity and an unholy attempt to depreciate and invalidate the supreme authority of the Oracles of God. All the attempts which have been made to explain the *rationale* of inspiration have done nothing toward simplifying the subject, rather have they tended to mystify. It is no easier to conceive how ideas without words could be imparted, than that Divinely revealed truths should be communicated by words. Instead of being diminished, the difficulty is increased. It is as logical to talk of a sum without figures or a tune without notes, as of a Divine revelation and communication without words. Instead of speculation, our duty is to receive and believe what the Scriptures say of themselves.

What the Bible teaches about its own inspiration is a matter *purely of Divine testimony*, and our business is simply to receive the testimony and not to speculate about or seek to pry into its *modus operandi*. Inspiration is as much a matter of Divine revelation as is justification by faith. Both stand equally on the authority of the Scriptures themselves, which must be the final court of appeal on this subject as on every question of revealed truth.

The teaching of the Bible concerning the inspiration of the Scriptures is clear and simple, and uniform throughout. Its writers were conscious that their utterances were a message from God in the highest meaning of the word. *"And the Lord said unto him [Moses], Who hath made man's mouth? or who maketh the dumb, or deaf, or the seeing, or the blind? Have not I the Lord? Now therefore go, and I will be with thy mouth, and teach thee what thou shalt say"* (Exodus 4:11–12). *"The Spirit of the Lord spake by me, and His word was in my tongue"* (2 Samuel 23:2). *"Then the Lord put forth His hand, and touched my mouth. and the Lord said unto* me, Behold, I have put My words in thy mouth" (Jeremiah 1:9). The above are only a sample of scores of similar passages which might be sighted.

What is predicted of the Scriptures themselves, demonstrates that they are entirely and absolutely the Word of God. *"The law of the Lord is perfect, converting the soul"* (Psalm 19:7)—this altogether excludes any place in the Bible for human infirmities and imperfections. *"Thy Word is very pure"* (Psalm 119:140), which cannot mean less than that the Holy Spirit so superintended the composition of the Bible and so "moved" its writers that all error has been excluded. *"Thy Word is true from the beginning"* (Psalm 119:160)—how this anticipated the assaults of the higher critics on the Book of Genesis, particularly on its opening chapters!

The teaching of the New Testament agrees with what we have quoted from the Old. *"Take ye no thought how or what thing ye shall answer, or what ye shall say: for the Holy Spirit shall teach you in the same hour what ye ought to say"* (Luke 12:11-12)—the disciples were the ones who spake, but it was the Holy Spirit who *"taught them what to say."* Could any language express more emphatically the most entire inspiration? And, if the Holy Spirit so controlled their utterances when in the presence of magistrates, is it conceivable that He would do less for them when they were communicating the mind of God to all future generations on things touching our eternal destiny? Assuredly not. *"But those things, which God before had showed by the mouth of all His prophets, that Christ should suffer, He hath so fulfilled"* (Acts 3:18). Here the Holy Spirit declares through Peter that it was *God* who had revealed by the mouth of all His prophets that Israel's Messiah must suffer before the glory should appear. "*But that I confess unto thee, that after the way which they call heresy, so worship I the God of my fathers, believing all things which are written in the law and in the prophets*" (Acts 24:14). These words clearly evidence the fact that the Apostle Paul had the utmost confidence in the authenticity of the entire contents of the Old Testament. "*And my speech and my preaching was not with enticing words of man's wisdom, but in demonstration of the Spirit and of power*" (1 Corinthians 2:4). Could any man have used such language as this unless he had been fully conscious that he was speaking the very words of God? "*For the prophecy came not in old time by the will of man: but holy men of God spake as they were moved by the Holy Ghost*" (2 Peter 1:21) Nothing could possibly be more explicit.

Dr. Gray has strikingly and forcefully stated the necessity of a *verbally* inspired Bible in the following language:—"An illustration the writer has often used will help to make this clear. A stenographer in a mercantile house was asked by his employer to write as follows:

"Gentlemen, we misunderstood your letter and will *now* fill your order."

Imagine the employer's surprise, however, when a little later this was set before him for his signature—

"Gentlemen, we misunderstood your letter and will *not* fill your order."

The mistake was only of a single letter, but it was entirely subversive of his meaning. And yet the thought was given clearly to the stenographer, and the words, too, for that matter, Moreover, the latter was capable and faithful, but he was human, and it is human to err. Had not his employer controlled his expression, down to the very letter, the thought intended to be conveyed would have failed of utterance." So, too, the Holy Spirit had to superintend the writing of the very letter of Scripture in order to guarantee its accuracy and inerrancy.

Many proofs might be given to show the Scriptures are verbally inspired. One line of demonstration appears in the literal and verbal fulfillment of many of the Old Testament prophecies. For example, God made known through Zechariah that the price which Judas should receive for his awful crime was *"thirty pieces of silver"* (Zechariah 11:12). Here, then, is a clear case where God communicated to one of the prophets not merely an abstract concept but a specific communication. And the above case is only one of many.

Another evidence of verbal inspiration is to be seen in the fact that *words* are used in Scripture with the most exact precision and discrimination. This is particularly noticeable in connection with the Divine titles. The names Elohim and Jehovah are found on the pages of the Old Testament several thousand times, but they are never employed loosely or used alternately. Each of these names has a definite significance and scope, and were we to substitute the one for the other, the beauty and perfection of a multitude of passages would be destroyed. To illustrate: the word *"God"* occurs throughout Genesis 1, but *"Lord God"* in Genesis 2. Were these two Divine titles reversed here, a flaw and blemish would be the consequence. *"God"* is the creatorial title, whereas *"Lord"* implies a covenant relationship and shows God's dealings with His own people. Hence, in Genesis 1, *"God"* is used, and in Genesis 2, *"Lord*

God" is employed, and throughout the rest of the Old Testament these two Divine titles are used discriminatively and in harmony with the meaning of their first mention. One or two other examples must suffice. "*And they went in unto Noah into the ark, two and two of all flesh, wherein is the breath of life. And they that went in, went in male and female of all flesh, as God had commanded him*" (Genesis 7:15)—"God" because it was the Creator commanding, with respect to His creatures, as such; but, in the remainder of the same verse, we read, "*and the Lord shut him in*" (Genesis 7:16), because God's action here toward Noah was based upon covenant relationship. When going forth to meet Goliath, David said, "*This day will the Lord deliver thee into mine hand* [because David was in covenant relationship with Him]; *and I will smite thee, and take thine head from thee; and I will give the carcasses of the host of the Philistines this day unto the fowls of the air, and to the wild beasts of the earth; that all the earth* [which was not in covenant relation with Him] *may know that there is a God in Israel. And all this assembly* [which were in covenant relationship with Him] *shall know that the Lord saveth not with sword and spear*" etc. (1 Samuel 17:46–47). Once more: "*And it came to pass, when the captains of the chariots saw Jehoshaphat, that they said, It is the king of Israel. Therefore they compassed about him to fight: but Jehoshaphat cried out, and the Lord helped him; and God moved them* [the Syrians] *to depart from him*" (2 Chronicles 18:31). And thus it is throughout the Old Testament.

The above line of argument might be extended indefinitely. There are upwards of fifty Divine titles in the Old Testament which are used more than once, each of which has a definite signification, each of which has its meaning hinted at in its *first* mention, and each of which is used subsequently in harmony with its original purport. They are never used loosely or interchangeably. In every place where they occur, there is a reason for each variation. Such titles are the Most High, the Almighty, the God of Israel, the God of Jacob, the Lord our Righteousness, etc., etc., are not used haphazardly, but in every case in harmony with their original meaning and as the best suited to the context. The same is true in connection with the names of our Lord in the New Testament. In some passages, He is referred to as Christ, in others as Jesus, Jesus Christ, Christ Jesus, Lord Jesus Christ. In every instance, there is a reason for each variation, and in every case, the Holy Spirit has seen that they are employed with uniform significance. The same is true of the various names given to the great adversary. In some places he is termed Satan, in others the devil etc., etc.; but the different terms are used with unerring precision throughout. A further illustration is furnished by the father of Joseph. In his earlier life, he was always termed Jacob, later he received the name of Israel, but after this, sometimes we read of Jacob and sometimes of Israel. Whatever is predicted of Jacob refers to the acts of the "old man;" whatever is postulated of Israel were the fruits of the "new man." When he doubted it was *Jacob* who doubted, when he believed God, it was *Israel* who exercised faith. Accordingly, we read, "*And when Jacob had made an end of commanding his sons, he gathered up his feet into the bed, and yielded up the ghost*" (Genesis 49:33). But in the next verse we are told, "*And Joseph commanded his servants the physicians to embalm his father: and the physicians embalmed Israel*" (Genesis 50:2)!! Here then we see the marvelous verbal precision and perfection of Holy Scripture.

The most convincing of all the proofs and arguments for the verbal inspiration of the Scriptures is the fact that the Lord Jesus Christ regarded them and treated them as such. He Himself submitted to their authority. When assaulted by Satan, three times He replied, "*It is written,*" (Matthew 4:4, 7, 10) and it is particularly to be noted that the point of each of His quotations and the force of each reply lay in a single word—"*Man shall not live by bread alone*" (v. 4) etc.; "*Thou shalt not tempt the Lord thy God;*" (v. 7) "*Thou shalt worship the Lord thy God, and him only shalt thou serve*" (v. 10). When tempted by the Pharisees, who asked Him, "*Is it lawful for a man to put away his wife for every cause?*" He answered, "*Have ye not read?*" etc. (Matthew 19:4–5). To the Sadducees, He said, "*Ye do err, not knowing the Scriptures*" (Matthew 22:29). On another occasion, He accused the Pharisees of "*Making the Word of God of none effect through their tradition*" (Mark 7:13). On another occasion, when speaking of the Word of God, He declared, "*The Scripture cannot be broken*" (John 10:35). Sufficient has been adduced to show that the Lord Jesus regarded the Scriptures as the Word of God in the most absolute sense. In view of this fact, let Christians beware of detracting in the smallest degree from the perfect and full inspiration of the Holy Scriptures.

14. Application of the Argument

What is our attitude towards God's Word? The knowledge that the Scriptures are inspired by the Holy Spirit involves definite obligations. Our conception of the authority of the Bible determines our attitude and measures our responsibility. If the Bible is a Divine revelation what follows?

We Need to Seek God's Forgiveness.

If it were announced upon reliable authority that on a certain date in the near future an angel from heaven would visit New York and would deliver a sermon upon the invisible world, the future destiny of man, or the secret of deliverance from the power of sin, what an audience he would command! There is no building in that city large enough to accommodate the crowd which would throng to hear him. If upon the next day, the newspapers were to give a verbatim report of his discourse, how eagerly it would be read! And yet, we have between the covers of the Bible not merely an angelic communication, but a Divine revelation. How great, then, is our wickedness if we undervalue and despise it! And yet we do.

We need to confess to God our sin of neglecting His Holy Word. We have time enough—we take time—to read the writings of fellow sinners, yet we have little or no time for the Holy Scriptures. The Bible is a series of Divine love letters, and yet many of God's people have scarcely broken the seals. God complained of old, "*I have written to him the great things of My law, but they were counted as a strange thing*" (Hosea 8:12). To neglect God's gift is to despise the Giver. To neglect God's Word is virtually to tell Him that He made a mistake in being at so much trouble to communicate it. To prefer the writings of man is to insult the Almighty. To say that human writings are more interesting is to impugn the wisdom of the Most High and is a terrible indictment against our own evil hearts. To neglect God's Word is to sin against its Author, for He has commanded us to read, study, and search it.

If the Bible is the Word of God, then—

It Is the Final Court of Appeal.

It is not a question of what I think, or of what anyone else thinks—it is, What saith the Scriptures? It is not a matter of what any church or creed teaches—it is, what teaches the Bible? God has spoken, and that ends the matter: "*Thy word is settled in heaven*" (Psalm 119:89). Therefore, it is for me to bow to His authority, to submit to His Word, to cease all quibbling and cry, "*Speak, Lord, for Thy servant heareth*" (1 Samuel 3:9). Because the Bible is *God's* Word, it is the final court of appeal in all things pertaining to doctrine, duty, and deportment.

This was the position taken by our Lord Himself. When tempted by Satan, He declined to argue with him, He refused to overwhelm him with the force of His superior wisdom, He scorned to crush him with a putting forth of His almighty power—"*It is written*" was His defense for each assault. At the beginning of His public ministry, when He went to Nazareth where most of His thirty years had been lived, He performed no wonderful miracle but entered the synagogue, read from the Prophet Isaiah and said, "*This day is this Scripture fulfilled in your ears*" (Luke 4:21). In His teaching upon the Rich Man and Lazarus, He insisted that "*If they hear not Moses and the prophets, neither will they be persuaded, though one rose from the dead*" (Luke 16:31)—thus signifying that the authority of the written Word is of greater weight and worth than the testimony and appeal of miracles. When vindicating before the Jews His claim of Deity (John 5) He appealed to the testimony of John the Baptist (v. 32), to His own works (v. 36), to the Father's own witness—at His baptism (v. 37), and then—as though they were the climax—He said—"*Search the Scriptures they are they which testify of Me*" (v. 39).

This was the position taken by the Apostles. When Peter would justify the speaking with other tongues, he appealed to the Prophet Joel (Acts 2:16). When seeking to prove to the Jews that Jesus of Nazareth was their Messiah, and that He had risen again from the dead, he appealed to the testimony of the Old Testament (Acts 2). When Stephen made his defense before the counsel he did little more than review the teaching of Moses and the prophets (Acts 7). When Saul and Barnabas set out on their first missionary journey they "*preached the Word of God in the synagogues of the Jews*" (Acts 13:5). In his Epistles, the Apostle continually pauses to ask—"*What saith the Scripture?*" (Romans 4:3)—if the Scripture gave a clear utterance upon the subject under discussion that ended the matter: against *their* testimony there was no appeal.

If the Bible is the Word of God then—

It Is the Ultimate Standard for Regulating Conduct.

How can man be just with God? or how can he be clean that is born of a woman? What must I do to be saved? Where is true and lasting peace and rest to be found? Such are some of the inquiries made by every honest and anxious soul. The reply is—Search the Scriptures: Look and see. How shall I best employ my time and talents? How shall I discover what is well-pleasing to my Maker? How am I to know what is the path of duty? And again the answer is—What teaches the Word of God?

No one who possesses a copy of the Bible can legitimately plead ignorance of God's will. The Scriptures leave us without excuse. A lamp has been provided for our feet and the pathway of righteousness is clearly marked out. A chart has been given to the sailors on time's sea, and it is their own fault if they fail to arrive at the heavenly port. In the day of judgment the Books will be opened and out of these Books men will be judge, and one of these Books will be the Bible. In His written Word, God has revealed His mind, expressed His will, communicated His requirements; and woe to the man or woman who takes not the necessary time to discover what these are.

If the Bible is the Word of God then—

It Is a Sure Foundation for Our Faith.

Man craves for certainty. Speculations and hypotheses are insufficient where eternal issues are at stake. When I come to lay my head upon my dying pillow, I want something surer than a "perhaps" to rest it upon. And thank God I have it. Where? In the Holy Scriptures. I know that my

Redeemer liveth. I know that I have passed from death unto life. I know that I shall be made like Christ and dwell with Him in glory throughout the endless ages of eternity. How do I know? Because *God's* Word says so, and I want nothing more.

The Bible gives forth no uncertain sound. It speaks with absolute assurance, dogmatism, and finality. Its promises are certain, for they are promises of Him who cannot lie. Its testimony is reliable, for it is the inerrant Word of the Living God. Its teachings are trustworthy, for they are a communication of the Omniscient. The believer then has a sure foundation on which to rest, an impregnable rock on which to build his hopes. For his present peace and for his future prospects he has a, "Thus saith *the Lord*," and that is sufficient.

If the Bible is the Word of God then—

It Has Unique Claims Upon Us.

A unique book deserves and demands unique attention. Like Job, we ought to be able to say, "I have esteemed the words of His mouth more than my necessary food" (23:12). If history teaches us anything at all, it teaches that those nations which have most honored God's Word have been most honored by God. And what is true of the nation is equally true of the family and of the individual. The greatest intellects of the ages have drawn their inspiration from the Scripture of Truth. The most eminent statesmen have testified to the value and importance of Bible study. Benjamin Franklin said: "Young man, my advice to you is that you cultivate an acquaintance with and firm belief in the Holy Scriptures, for this is your certain interest." Thomas

Jefferson gave it as his opinion, "I have said and always will say that the studious perusal of the Sacred Volume will make better citizens, better fathers, and better husbands."

When the late Queen Victoria was asked the secret of England's greatness, she took down a copy of the Scriptures, and pointing to the Bible she said, "That Book explains the power of Great Britain." Daniel Webster once affirmed, "If we abide by the principles taught in the Bible, our country will go on prospering and to prosper; but, if we and our posterity neglect its instructions and authority, no man can tell how sudden a catastrophe may overwhelm us and bury all our glory in profound obscurity. The Bible is the Book of all others for lawyers as well as divines, and I pity the man who cannot find in it a rich supply of thought and rule of conduct."

When Sir Walter Scott lay dying he summoned to his side his man in waiting and said, "Read to me out of the Book." Which book? Answered his servant. "There is only one Book," was the dying man's response—"The Bible!" The Bible is the Book to live by and the Book to die by. Therefore read it to be wise, believe it to be safe, practice it to be holy. As another has said: "Know it in the head, store it in the heart, show it in the life, sow it in the world."

"All Scripture is given by inspiration of God, and is profitable for doctrine, for reproof, for correction, for instruction in righteousness: that the man of God may be perfect, thoroughly furnished unto all good works" (2 Timothy 3:16–17).

www.ingramcontent.com/pod-product-compliance
Lightning Source LLC
Chambersburg PA
CBHW012106090526
44592CB00019B/2674